# MONSTERS

## OF THE

# IVY
# LEAGUE

# MONSTERS
## OF THE
# IVY
# LEAGUE

## A GALLERY OF ELITE ASSHOLES

# Steve Radlauer and Ellis Weiner

*Drawings by Randy Jones*

LITTLE, BROWN AND COMPANY
New York   Boston   London

Little, Brown and Company
Hachette Book Group
1290 Avenue of the Americas, New York, NY 10104
littlebrown.com

First edition: April 2017

Little, Brown and Company is a division of Hachette Book Group, Inc. The Little, Brown and Company name and logo are trademarks of Hachette Book Group, Inc.

The publisher is not responsible for websites (or their content) that are not owned by the publisher.

The Hachette Speakers Bureau provides a wide range of authors for speaking events. To find out more, go to hachettespeakersbureau.com or call (866) 376-6591.

ISBN 978-0-316-46529-8
LCCN 2016962006

10 9 8 7 6 5 4 3 2 1

LSC-C

Printed in the United States of America

*To the memory of our introducer, Eliot Wald*

# Contents

# CONTENTS

# Introduction

In America, higher education (meaning, education even higher than so-called high school) has, over the past generation, become a topic of immense controversy. Everything about it — its cost, its utility, the political atmosphere on its campuses, the working conditions of its faculty, the social and sexual behavior of its students — has come under intense scrutiny.

An undergraduate degree, once esteemed as a prize available only to the (white, Christian, male) "Joe College" privileged, is now considered as basic, universal, and unremarkable as a high school diploma. A college education, formerly regarded as a ticket to the next-higher rung up the socioeconomic ladder (at least!), is now derided as a way for twentysomethings to incur crippling debt while pursuing a diploma of limited usefulness in today's deteriorating job market.

Meanwhile, the college campus has become a debased cartoon of its former self, a place of unbridled sexual activity and rampant sexual abuse, where professors don't teach (that job is left to underpaid teaching assistants and adjuncts), students don't study (they regard themselves not as apprentices but as customers), and open inquiry is hamstrung by "political correctness" and free speech constrained by the need for "trigger warnings."

But throughout the most heated debates, as parents' tuition costs soar and students' return on investment plummets, one thing has remained constant: the prestige and respectability accorded the Ivy League.

What is the Ivy League? Contrary to what its name implies, it is not a collection of amateur gardeners. Nor does the term stand for "good colleges." Or "good colleges in the northeastern United States." It doesn't mean "Harvard, Yale, Georgetown, Princeton, and a few others."

In fact—and this will surprise those to whom this news comes as a surprise—the Ivy League is actually *a bunch of football teams.*

Okay, basketball and other sports, too. In any case, that's why it says "league." Get it? It's an athletic conference consisting of eight institutions: Brown University, Columbia University, Cornell University, Dartmouth College, Harvard University, the University of Pennsylvania, Princeton University, and Yale University. All except Cornell were born before the American Revolution. And while "Ivy" and "Ivy League" appeared as casual references to certain schools as far back as the 1930s, the actual Ivy League was formed in 1954 to formalize the sporting relationships among these eight schools—relationships that in some cases went back to the 1800s.

But who(m) are we kidding? Nobody applies to these schools because they are a gateway to the NFL or the NBA. *Au contraire:* The term "Ivy League education" refers to the gold standard in American pedagogy. The Ivies are *the best colleges in the country,* where the lucky student may avail him- or herself not only of *the finest education available,* but, equally important, *the best future contacts for their budding careers.**

The schools in the Ivy League are exclusive, expensive, and

---

* Well, not the *only* best. There are, of course, other prestigious schools *not* in the Ivy League, including Stanford, the University of Chicago, Williams, Amherst, Bob Jones (just kidding), MIT, NYU, UCLA, and [your favorite non-Ivy school here].

the subject of a young lifetime's worth of achievement anxiety and test-prep frenzy. If you are an Ivy-aspiring high school student, getting into one will likely require prodigious feats of book-learning, test-taking, and extracurricular-activity-doing hitherto unknown to mortal teenagers.

You may, for example, have spent the summer between sophomore and junior year studying the bassoon, in Spanish, in Paraguay, in order to be able to sit before the Princeton admissions lady and, when asked to tell her something about yourself, reply, "I spent last summer studying the bassoon, in Spanish, in Paraguay." You may have acquired two weeks of "enrichment" during freshman year's spring break by working as a line cook in a Turkish refugee camp. You may have won a plaid belt in caber tossing by age eleven. In your spare time, you may have sought (and won) first prize in the school science fair by teaching calculus to a flatworm.

To you, as to your peers, childhood has been a series of auditions, with ever-increasing stakes, and all with one goal in mind: acceptance into an Ivy League school. If you get in, you'll be relieved, if exhausted. If you don't, you'll be suicidal. Perhaps you've already received the coveted Thick Packet of Welcome — or, alas, the dreaded Skinny Envelope of Rejection.

*Whichever the case,* you're going to want to read what follows.

So will your parents. Naturally, everything they've done for you since your birth — the encouraging, the paying, the attending, the schlepping to practice and rehearsals and lessons and games, the haranguing, the tutor-hiring, the homework-checking — has been a selfless act of dedication for your benefit alone. And even if it hasn't — even if their egos and self-images have been wrapped up in your academic achievement — so what? Why shouldn't they, in taking pride in you, take pride in themselves? Similarly, if your rejection by the Ivies makes you question your worth as a human being, fear for your future, and despair of existence itself, why shouldn't they feel the same?

They do. Or they will. It is for them, too, that this book has been written. Even the Sure Thing families who take acceptance for granted (Ivy grads whose kids are all but guaranteed legacy admission; rich people identified by college development departments as likely sources of handsome donations; rich people whose surnames already adorn a campus hockey rink or library) and, yes, even students already enrolled in one of the Ivies, will benefit from the following review of some of the Ivies' "work product," faculty members, donors, and founders.

Because (spoiler alert) it's not all Nobel Prizes and Wall Street fortunes.

In fact, your precious Ivy League has inflicted on American society some of the worst killers, criminals, and moral reprobates in its killer-criminal-and-moral-reprobate-rich history. An Ivy education doesn't *force* you to become a hideous person, but it doesn't necessarily prevent it, either. And yet, oddly enough, none of these facts are disclosed at Harvard's get-acquainted dinners or during Penn's campus tours. No one, during a Whiffenpoof concert or at halftime of the Columbia-Brown game, reminisces about sociopathic alumni.

Why? Who knows. In any case, that's why we're here. What follows is a smart-shopper warning to those applying, a count-your-blessings consolation to those who have been rejected, and a watch-your-back caution to those already attending. Sure, every college and university produces its share of monsters. But it takes these eight golden institutions to produce genuine Ivy League monsters. Read and learn.

# Key

**Names in Bold**: Ivy monsters with entries in this book

NAMES IN SMALL CAPS: Ivy monsters who are listed in the Beneath Contempt section, which appears after the collection of the above boldface monsters

## SYMBOLS

| | | | |
|---|---|---|---|
| **AS** Anti-Semite | | **Ms** Misogynist |
| **A** Authoritarian | | **M** Murderer |
| **B** Boob | | **P** Plagiarist |
| **Bu** Bully | | **Ped** Pederast |
| **CP** Classification Pending | | **R** Racist |
| **DN** Dangerous Narcissist | | **RL** Religious Loon |
| **DoE** Defender of Evil | | **RWN** Right-Wing Nutbar |
| **Dg** Demagogue | | **S** Scammer |
| **DPo** Disgrace to Position | | **SK** Serial Killer |
| **DPr** Disgrace to Profession | | **SxF** Sex Fiend |
| **DT** Domestic Terrorist | | **SL** Shameless Liar |
| **D** Douche | | **Slv** Slaver |
| **EB** Eugenics Buff | | **Tr** Traitor |
| **E** Eugenicist | | **T** Thief |
| **FF** Financial Fraudster | | **UI** Useful Idiot |
| **GB** Greedy Bastard | | **VL** Vulgar Lout |
| **H** Homophobe | | **WC** War Criminal |
| **KP** Kiddie-Porner | | **Wgr** Warmonger |
| **LL** Lowlife | | **WS** White Supremacist |
| **MM** Megalomaniac | | **W** Wimp |

MONSTERS
OF THE
IVY
LEAGUE

# Dr. Keith Ablow

*BS, Brown University*

When Brown University dies and goes to heaven, and stands before St. Peter to account for its sins and misdeeds, it's going to have some explaining to do about Dr. Keith Ablow.

Ablow graduated magna cum laude from Brown in 1983 and followed up with an MD from Johns Hopkins Med School in 1987. Impressive! He then went on to write for numerous publications, to coauthor a book with noted sobbing-conspiracy-maniac Glenn Beck, to host his own television talk show, and to attain a lucrative career as the official psychiatric spokesperson for such penetrating, not-at-all-intellectually-disgraceful shows on Fox News as *Fox & Friends, The 5,* and *The O'Reilly Factor.*

In so doing, he:

- Asserted that the Korean-language song "Gangnam Style" was "without intelligible words," and thus "without reality, feeling, and meaning," and that, therefore, watching it "is like taking a drug."
- Suggested—speaking from a perch "deep inside the president's psyche"—that President Obama, during the Ebola outbreak in West Africa, "may" want us to suffer an Ebola onslaught, too. "How can you protect a country you don't like?" Ablow pondered.
- Declared—in an interview with Lou Dobbs on the Fox Business Channel—that President Obama had "severed himself from all core emotions." His use of the word "core" says "I am

a scientist and this is scientific fact." No wonder Obama's public displays of sadness (at funerals), irritation (with Republicans), and pride (in his family) look so severed.

But Ablow has done more than offer televised saloon-drunk ravings as psychiatric insight. He's written them, too. Who else could have given us, in "Men Should Be Allowed to Veto Abortions":*

I believe that in those cases in which a man can make a credible claim that he is the father of a developing child in utero, in which he could be a proper custodian of that child, and in which he is willing to take full custody of that child upon its delivery, that the pregnant woman involved should not have the option to abort and should be civilly liable, and possibly criminally liable, for psychological suffering and wrongful death should she proceed to do so.

If, after the child is born, the father decides to bag the whole full-custody deal and skip out, who would be responsible for the baby's care? Should the mother be prosecuted for manslaughter if she miscarries and the poor, psychologically suffering father is rendered distraught? Dr. Ablow doesn't tell us.

Then again, in Ablow's world men typically get a little more slack than women. Certainly Newt Gingrich does. Behold what the psychiatrist wrote about Gingrich's serial infidelities and serial marriages:

You can take any moral position you like about men and women who cheat while married, but there simply is no cor-

---

* Which he wrote for *The Huffington Post*.

relation, whatsoever—from a psychological perspective—between whether they can remain true to their wedding vows and whether they can remain true to the Oath of Office.

Some people—let's call them "women"—might find this statement to be of dubious validity. Ablow explains:

> ...here's what one interested in making America stronger can reasonably conclude—psychologically—from Mr. Gingrich's behavior during his three marriages:
>
> 1) Three women have met Mr. Gingrich and been so moved by his emotional energy and intellect that they decided they wanted to spend the rest of their lives with him.
>
> 2) Two of these women felt this way even though Mr. Gingrich was already married.
>
> 3) One of them felt this way even though Mr. Gingrich was already married for the second time, was not exactly her equal in the looks department and had a wife (Marianne) who wanted to make his life without her as painful as possible.

**Conclusion:** When three women want to sign on for life with a man who is now running for president, I worry more about whether we'll be clamoring for a third Gingrich term, not whether we'll want to let him go after one.

Ablow has deep thoughts about the Holocaust, too. He wrote—perhaps employing crackpot-doctor professional courtesy—that **Dr. Ben Carson** was right when Carson said that "if guns had not been confiscated from Jews then Hitler would have had more trouble orchestrating the Holocaust." Ablow, feigning intellectual honesty, goes on:

Granted, I was not there. Granted, hindsight is 20/20. But it turns out it was a bad idea for any Jew to have turned over a gun. It was a bad idea for any Jew to have boarded a train.

What's his point? Ablow wants to pander to gun nuts:

The wisest answer to a government that insists its citizens disarm is, "Over my dead body." It would seem to be the end of any discussion and the beginning of active, heroic resistance. Because it is very hard to imagine that disempowering citizens by having them render themselves defenseless can lead to anything good. It is very likely a sign that the culture has fallen ill and that an epidemic of enslavement of one kind or another is on the horizon.

There is, of course, more, including Ablow's claim that the change in California legal statutes substituting the word "spouse" for "husband" and "wife" means that people will be allowed to marry their dogs.

Could the success of Keith Ablow be a sign that the culture has fallen ill? Perhaps. Regardless, let's just end with what Dr. Jeffrey Lieberman, chairman of psychiatry at Columbia University's College of Physicians and Surgeons, said*—from a psychological perspective—about Fox News's hack-shrink for hire:

It is shameful and unfortunate that he is given a platform by Fox News or any other media organization. Basically he is a narcissistic self-promoter of limited and dubious expertise.

---

* To the Associated Press in 2014.

# Louis Agassiz

*Harvard University Professor* ★ *Cornell University Lecturer*

By the time the Swiss-born Jean Louis Rodolphe Agassiz reached the age of thirty, in 1837, he was already an eminent scientist: an ichthyologist (fish man), paleontologist (fossil man), and the first to propose that vast swaths of Europe had once been covered by ice (geology and glaciology man). Man, what a man!

He sailed to the United States in 1846 to study the New World's fish, fossils, and rocks, and to present a lecture series entitled (spoiler alert) "The Plan of Creation as Shown in the Animal Kingdom." Several prestigious American institutions, brandishing thick wallets and offering impressive academic appointments, immediately went a-courting this charismatic European star scientist. Harvard, looking to rebrand itself from a modest little college for the production of clergymen into a heavyweight university, won his heart,* anointing him professor of zoology and geology, and, for good measure, launching the Lawrence Scientific School (now the John A. Paulson†  School of Engineering and Applied Sciences), with Agassiz as chief.

---

\* Cornell, too, won a little piece of that heart, and brought Agassiz on as a "nonresident lecturer."

† Paulson is the Harvard alum (MBA, natch) hedge-fund guy who profited — to the tune of $15 billion — from the housing meltdown in the first decade of the 21st century.

An impressive researcher, writer, collector of natural specimens, institution builder (he founded Harvard's Museum of Comparative Zoology), as well as a leading educator (many of his students became influential teachers and researchers), Agassiz profoundly influenced the development of American science. But there was a problem. Several, actually.

Louis Agassiz was a racist.*

And he was, to put it calmly, religious. He took Genesis literally, at least as it applied to the origin of fair-skinned humans and their animal buddies. In a word — although the word hadn't been coined yet — he was a creationist. He wrote profusely on the subject of "polygenism," the theory that God created whites and blacks as separate species, with very different physical attributes, intellectual capabilities, and so on. Whites, of course, were superior to blacks in all ways, because that's how God rolls. This cast of mind led him to abominate his contemporary Darwin and cast aspersions on the theory of evolution.

Aside from incessantly writing and lecturing about black people's inferiority, Agassiz went to the trouble of demeaning them whenever possible. He hired photographers in the United States and Brazil to take pictures of naked slaves and other black people — "specimens" — in humiliating poses. And of course he did what he could to keep blacks (not to mention Italians and Jews) from enrolling at Harvard.

To recap: Agassiz was a Bible-belting, science-denying, hate-dripping racist crackpot who leveraged his legitimate scientific standing and Harvard authority to foist twisted, backward,

---

* Before crossing the Atlantic Agassiz had never seen a black person. Seeing them freaked him out. In a letter to his mother, he complained about their lips, teeth, hair, knees, hands, and overall degeneracy. Later, he lectured a no-doubt receptive audience in Charleston, South Carolina, that "the brain of the Negro is that of the imperfect brain of a seven months' infant in the womb of a White." He offered no scientific evidence to support this assertion.

utterly unscientific views on the world (and pave the way for what we now call "scientific racists" like **William Z. Ripley** and **Madison Grant**) while throwing shade at the most important scientific theory of the nineteenth century and its creator, Charles Darwin.

By the time he shuffled off this mortal coil,* in 1873, he was unquestionably the nation's foremost scientist. Things were named for him, including several species, a big chunk of Canadian landscape that was once a glacial lake, and an elementary school near Harvard that in turn gave its name — his name — to the surrounding neighborhood. Agassiz's genuine scientific work is undisputed to this day. His reputation as an all-around human being has not fared so well.†

Here's a fine example of this. Stephen Jay Gould‡ writes a book, *The Mismeasure of Man,* that includes a great deal of material confirming just how much of a racist Agassiz was. A student at the lovely, diverse Agassiz School in Cambridge reads the book and is scandalized to learn the true character of the man behind his school's name. The student goes public with the issue and finds that many others, kids and adults alike, are equally outraged. A local movement arises, culminating in an official name change in 2002.

Now it's called the Maria L. Baldwin School, after the woman who was the institution's beloved principal from 1889 to 1922. She, unlike Agassiz, is understood to have been a thoroughly good and decent person.

As you may have guessed, Maria L. Baldwin was black.

---

* His final reward? Most likely (if one subscribes to an Agassiz-style eschatology) eternal damnation in the fire-lake of hell under the steady, searing gaze of Lucifer.

† From the perspective of regular people, that is. To creationists, he's a fucking god.

‡ Who was — get ready — the Agassiz Professor of Zoology at Harvard.

# Samuel F. Alito

*BA, Princeton University* ★ *JD, Yale University*

In January 2016, when the Republican Party candidates for president assembled in Houston for a debate, **Ted Cruz** lamented the GOP's history of placing jurists on the Supreme Court. "The reality is, Democrats bat about 1.000," he said. "Just about everyone they put on the court votes exactly as they want. Republicans have batted worse than .500. More than half of the people we put on the court have been a disaster."

Cruz was complaining about the occasional semi-"liberal" votes of John Roberts, Anthony Kennedy, the notoriously independent David Souter, and even, now and then, **Antonin Scalia**. Cruz—the only politician in our lifetime famous for being despised as much by his own party as by the opposing party—couldn't have been too crazy about Sandra Day O'Connor, either.

Now, you and we might ascribe those justices' deviation from the GOP party line to the fact that, as the saying goes, "reality has a liberal bias." Meaning, the liberal position on certain issues is so obviously the fair, just, and correct one that even career conservatives are forced to acknowledge it from time to time, if through legally gritted teeth.

But not all of them.

**Clarence Thomas** dependably hews to the far-right line. And who can blame him? Already knowing how you'll vote allows you to take a nap on the bench during oral arguments and still wake up refreshed and revived, unconcerned about what was said in your mental absence.

And then there's Samuel F. Alito. Dubbed "Scalito" for his Mini-Me lockstep agreement with the older, more senior Scalia, Alito has proved to be the conservative's conservative — except when a Democrat is president, at which time he gets a little cute with the rulings.

What kind of man is Alito? He's the kind of man who as a kid was a big Phillies fan, played second base in Little League, and dreamed of a career in Major League Baseball — *as the commissioner.* When serving on the Third Circuit Court of Appeals, he ruled in favor of cops who, armed with a warrant allowing them to search a suspected meth dealer, decided also to strip-search the suspect's ten-year-old daughter. Don't act surprised. The Founders would have done the same thing, if they had been there and if they had known what meth was.

Also while on the Third Circuit Court, Alito held *against* people alleging race, age, gender, and disability discrimination; *in favor of* an individual's right to possess a fucking machine gun; and *for* imposing strict waiting periods for women seeking abortions.

This has been his pattern: to defend the rights of institutions at the expense of individuals (unless they're white Catholic men). He voted *for* Citizens United, supporting corporate "personhood" and permitting unlimited expenditure of cash in federal elections. He held *in favor of* Hobby Lobby and that company's "religious" objection to paying for its employees' contraception. He sided *with* the majority in *Ledbetter v. Goodyear,* which made it harder for women to bring unequal-pay lawsuits.

Confused? It's simple: corporations are "people," and have an unlimited right to express themselves with money, as though an unlimited ability to influence an election isn't the very definition of corruption. People, however (especially women-type people), aren't entirely people, and have circumscribed rights to control their own bodies, to be free of restrictions imposed by employers' religious beliefs, and to sue for equal treatment.

Alito was a big promoter of the "unitary executive" theory, the notion that the president had virtually unlimited powers and could exercise them via "signing statements." He held in favor of the Pentagon in one Guantánamo-related case, and with **George W. Bush**, who nominated him for the Supreme Court in 2005, in another.

And yet, once Barack Obama became president, Alito found himself concerned about presidential overreach. He held in favor of two challenges to the Affordable Care Act and expressed dismay at Obama's exercise of power with regard to immigration and the regulation of greenhouse gases.

In sum, Samuel Alito is a principled conservative who doesn't let being principled impede his ability to be, if not always conservative, certainly dependably Republican. He's not the opera buffa villain that Scalia was, but he is nonetheless capable of scowling and sighing and looking pissy while hearing arguments he doesn't like, and mouthing "Not true" during one of Obama's State of the Union addresses.

He would have made a lousy MLB commissioner, too.

# Amy Bishop

*PhD, Harvard University*

**SK**

Amy Bishop was born in 1965 in Massachusetts. She attended the unpleasantly-but-perhaps-appropriately-named Braintree High School and obtained her undergraduate degree at Northeastern University. She then went on to acquire a PhD in genetics at Harvard. That can't be easy — and, indeed, Bishop was rather proud of her accomplishment. Perhaps *too* proud; she frequently introduced herself to strangers as "Dr. Amy Bishop, Harvard-trained." The "Dr." part would have been off-putting enough. The "Harvard-trained" part opens a door to a world of crazy.

So it was that, on February 12, 2010, Harvard-trained Dr. Amy Bishop was attending a routine meeting of the biology department at the University of Alabama in Huntsville (UAH). She had, months earlier, been informed that she had been denied tenure, which meant that the university would soon be letting her go. Perhaps for this reason — or who knows? — she pulled out a 9-millimeter handgun and started shooting. In the end, three people were killed and three others wounded. When apprehended, Bishop murmured that she didn't know what had happened and "wasn't there."

Of course, she *was* there, just as she was there, in her family's home in (again) Braintree in 1986, when she was twenty-one and killed her brother Seth with a shotgun. She fired the gun twice, once into her bedroom wall, and once into Seth's chest. She and her mother claimed it was an accident, and so it was ruled — although eyebrows were raised when it was discovered that after the shooting she had racked the weapon, ejecting the spent shell and feeding a new one into the chamber. (We don't know about you, but when we accidentally shoot someone, the first thing we do is drop the weapon in dismay. We don't reload.)

Bishop, a second cousin of writer John Irving, was also an amateur novelist with three (unpublished) books to her credit. She was in a writers' club in Ipswich, Massachusetts, in the 1990s, where fellow club members described her as being smart but "abrasive," apt to invoke her Harvard degree to boost her novelist bona fides and constantly insisting that she was "entitled to praise."

It's all terrible. But surely, between the brother and the three UAH victims, that's all...right?

Well...there's also the Pipe Bomb Incident.

In 1993, Paul Rosenberg was a professor at Harvard Medical School. He was also Bishop's supervisor at the Children's Hospital neurobiology lab. Bishop was concerned that she was going to receive a negative evaluation from Rosenberg. On November 30 she quit her position as Rosenberg's researcher. On December 19, opening the mail, Rosenberg came upon a package bearing six suspiciously uncanceled stamps. Having recently attended a seminar on letter bombs (discussing, among other Harvard grads, **The Unabomber**), Rosenberg summoned the bomb squad, which determined that the package would have exploded in the scientist's face had he opened it.

Was this Bishop's doing? Perhaps, aided by her milquetoast-nerd husband, James (called "Jimmy Junior" by everyone except his hoity-toity wife) Anderson? According to case notes at the Bureau of Alcohol, Tobacco, and Firearms, Anderson said that he wanted to get back at Rosenberg, to "shoot him, bomb him, stab him," or perhaps "strangle" him. But talk is cheap, and due to lack of evidence, no charges were filed.

"Okay," you find yourself thinking, "This poor woman was obviously mentally or emotionally damaged — a borderline personality, maybe — and it's enough already. Just don't tell me she punched a woman in the International House of Pancakes."

Sorry. That, too. In 2002, in Peabody, Massachusetts, Bishop grew outraged when another customer got the last booster seat,* stormed over to her, and began to rant and scream and curse. When that proved unavailing, she slugged the lady in the head, screaming, "I am Dr. Amy Bishop!" Bishop pleaded guilty to misdemeanor assault and disorderly conduct. She received probation.

Eight years later she changed her plea in the Alabama murder case from not guilty to guilty when relatives of the UAH victims indicated that they opposed the death penalty. On September 24, 2010, Harvard-trained Dr. Amy Bishop was sentenced to life in prison without possibility of parole.

---

* Bishop is — and we can barely stand to type this — the mother of four (4!) children.

# William Bradford Bishop, Jr.

*BA, Yale University*

Brad Bishop graduated from Yale in 1959, collected a couple of MAs—in Italian from Middlebury, in African Studies from UCLA—got married, and took a job in counterintelligence for the US Army. Later, with his espionage experience and five languages plus English, he went to work for the State Department. There were many overseas postings in Africa and Europe. He did some more graduate work, this time at the University of Florence, in Italy. Finally, this Ivy League cold warrior came home to State Department headquarters in Washington, DC, as an assistant division chief. He, his wife, their three sons, and his mother lived together in swank, pleasant Bethesda, Maryland.

Bloodcurdling, isn't it? And yet our story is only beginning.

In 1976 Bishop learned that he would not get the promotion he was expecting. He was disappointed. Why wouldn't he be, with his Yale pedigree, his languages, his advanced degrees, and his record of service to his country? So he did what any of us would have done in a similar situation: he left work early, cleaned out his bank account, bought a small sledgehammer, a shovel, and a pitchfork, gassed up his station wagon and filled a gasoline can, went home, brutally bludgeoned his wife, kids, and mother with the sledge, packed their bodies into the station wagon, drove six hours to a swamp in North Carolina, dug a shallow hole, dumped the bodies, emptied the gasoline can, and started a big fire.

Excessive? Perhaps. Like we said: he was disappointed. Apart from that, who knows why he did it? One wants to confront the man and say, "Don't they teach you in Ivy League colleges not to massacre your family?" Although maybe they do, and his instruction just didn't take. In any case, as a character in Jean Renoir's classic film *The Rules of the Game* says, "The awful thing about life is this: everyone has their reasons."

Whatever Bishop's reasons were, he kept them to himself. He did his thing, and then he disappeared. As of this writing, William Bradford Bishop is still on the FBI's Most Wanted list. Over the years he's allegedly been spotted in England, Sweden, Switzerland, Italy, Belgium...let's just say "somewhere in downtown Europe." Which is to say, he may have been spotted but he's never been captured—a fact that speaks well of the tradecraft of our nation's espionage service. Forging passports and birth certificates is not that big a deal for a former spy; with those, along with dyed hair and a grown or shaved-off beard, he could be anywhere. He could be in Africa. He could be studying odontology at the Université de Montpellier. (*Somebody* must be. Why not Bishop?) He could be long dead.

Which raises the question: Might there be a special, ultra-exclusive, highly coveted, ivy-bedecked chamber of hell? If you end up there, reader, ask for Brad Bishop, and get back to us.

# Jason Bohn

*BA, Columbia University ★ MA, Columbia University*

M

Most Ivy League monsters are accustomed to doing whatever they want with few negative consequences—that's why you go to an Ivy League school, after all. What's the *point* of sitting through those lectures and reading those texts and writing those papers and taking those exams if you can't sanction the secret bombing of an entire country or get rich watching the US economy have a heart attack? Still, occasionally one golden Ivy grad will cross a line. It might be the line marked "Don't kick, stomp, and torture people," and then—who knows why? life can be so unfair—society will be obligated to retaliate.

After earning a bachelor's and a master's degree from Columbia, Jason Bohn went on to law school at the University of Florida. There he met and fell in love with a smart, beautiful Kentucky native, Danielle Thomas, who was working on her MBA. She apparently loved him in return. They were an ambi-

tious couple, and after receiving their degrees they moved to an apartment in Astoria, Queens. Both appeared to be on the fast track to New York fabulosity—she with a job as a financial analyst at Weight Watchers, he as a contract attorney for Goldman Sachs, Google, AOL, and other companies.

Unfortunately, Ms. Thomas soon learned that despite his impressive credentials, her boyfriend was prone to fits of uncontrollable rage — so uncontrollable that in early June 2012 she was forced to flee to a battered women's shelter. She obtained a restraining order to keep Bohn away, but later that month, for reasons known only to her, she found herself back in the apartment with him. There he kicked, stomped, and tortured her for an hour and a half before strangling her to death.

The tabloids ridiculed the only argument his lawyer put forth at the trial: as a child Bohn had been abandoned by his mother, which led to the extreme mental condition that caused him to kill the woman he loved. The jury didn't buy it, either. To quote the *New York Daily News* of March 5, 2014:

> A loathsome law school grad was convicted Wednesday of beating and choking his girlfriend to death in a horrific attack....Jason Bohn, 35, was found guilty of first-degree murder for snuffing the life out of Danielle Thomas, 27, inside their Astoria, Queens, apartment in June 2012.

Over to the *New York Post* for Bohn's punishment:

> Convicted Ivy League killer Jason Bohn blubbered his way through a sentencing in Queens... where a judge hit him with a maximum of life behind bars with no chance for parole.

This may have been the only occasion in the history of the world in which an account of torture and murder included the word "blubbered." Then again, it's the *New York Post,* so maybe they do that all the time. Even in sports articles.

In any case, Bohn's new roommates for life will no doubt enjoy this detail from the UK's *Daily Mail:*

Though he never shed a tear in court over the merciless 90-minute torture attack during which the helpless victim begged for her life, Bohn bawled so hard during Judge Michael Aloise's sentencing that Bohn's nose started to bleed.

Poor baby.

# Gary Bremer

*BA,\* Dartmouth College*

KP

Gary Bremer was the valedictorian of Dartmouth's class of 1984. Great! Twenty-two years later, when he was forty-five, he was arrested for having copious quantities of child pornography on his computer. Not great!

At Bremer's trial in Connecticut Superior Court, the judge proclaimed the pictures "vile and disgusting in every sense of the word" and sentenced him to two years in prison plus five years' probation; the judge also prohibited Bremer from having any contact with minors or with the Internet, and placed him on the Connecticut sex-offender registry for ten years.

For a guy smart enough to get into Dartmouth and to graduate ahead of all the others smart enough to get into the class of '84, he was kind of stupid. Why do we say that? Because he did a number of stupid things:

- Stupid thing no. 1: He claimed he didn't know he was breaking the law when he downloaded hundreds of pictures of children and babies being sexually assaulted by adults.
- Stupid thing no. 2: He put prurient titles, like "child porn" and "Lolita," on his pictures.
- Stupid thing no. 3: He claimed that in 2002 he decided to kick the habit, drop his Internet connection, and get rid of his laptop—by pawning it, without first wiping the hard

---

\* Dartmouth perversely calls it an AB. So do Harvard and some of the others. We think this is just wrong.

21

drive clean or driving a railroad spike through it. When he didn't return to claim it, the pawnshop fired up the computer to check it out. Guess what they found.

- Stupid thing no. 4: Bremer, through his lawyer, claimed the oldest excuse in the, uh, book, which was that he was planning to *write* some kind of book and was using the vile and disgusting material for research. "Artistic purposes" happens to be an accepted defense for being a kiddie-porn enthusiast in Connecticut. It didn't work.
- Stupid thing no. 5: After entering his guilty plea, Bremer apparently forgot his "artistic" defense and said he didn't know why he had all those pictures of adults sexually assaulting children and babies.

Bremer collected his illegal pictures from the Internet and never, as his lawyer put it, "crossed the line from fantasy to reality," i.e., never had any contact with an actual child. Great! Well, adequate, anyway.

The National Center for Missing and Exploited Children identified at least three of the children in Gary Bremer's collection as victims of sexual assault, perpetrated by people who did have contact with actual children but in all likelihood were not Dartmouth valedictorians.

# The Brown Family

*Brown University Benefactors*

To a busy, highly educated, social-media-savvy, staring-at-smartphone-while-skateboarding, thoroughly up-to-date individual of present-day now, Rhode Island may not seem a likely place to have been deeply involved in the slave trade. After all, it's not in the South — it's in New England, for gosh sakes! — it's quaint, it seems kind of nice, it's extremely small. But check out this bogus eighteenth-century tweet: ZOUNDS! RI AT HEART OF SLAVE-SHIPPING & -SHIP-BUILDING INDUSTRY, W/BIG SLAVE MARKETS, LOTSA SLAVES ON FARMS, SWEATSHOPS, EVERYWHERE!#PROFIT

For Rhode Islanders, the slave trade* was *the* hot new business opportunity, the virtual-reality goggles of the era. From the early 1700s to the early 1800s, Rhode Islanders invested† in over 1,000 slave ships, wresting more than 106,000 human beings from their African homelands and…well, you don't need us to fill in the gory details.

So successful was slaving that it took over — *became* — the economy of Rhode Island.‡ There were boatbuilders and carpenters,

---

* And not just any slave trade, but the famous "triangle" trade: grab people in Africa, sail to the Caribbean, trade some shackled people for sugar and molasses, sail to Providence and/or other ports, sell the remaining people and distill the sugar and molasses into rum, schlep the rum to Africa to trade for more slaves, etc.

† Everyone was doing it, not just the rich. It was as mainstream as your IRA.

‡ At times up to 90 percent of all slaves imported to North America were conveyed by ships owned and built by the citizens of this shrimpy little state. "Li'l Rhodie" consistently punched above its weight slave-trade-wise.

sailmakers, blacksmiths, caulkers, rope makers and riggers, shackle-and-chain artisans, and all the other specialists required for the construction of seaworthy vessels with belowdeck dungeons. There were provisioners, supplying the ships with victuals. There were captains, sailors, cooks. And there was the rum industry,* an integral piece of the triangle-trade puzzle, which employed distillery workers and laborers, lumberjacks who felled trees, teamsters who transported the trees, and coopers who fashioned the wood into barrels. Don't forget the hoteliers, housekeeping staff, and, presumably, prostitutes, all mandatory components of thriving seaports everywhere. It was a sprawling enterprise, and if you lived there you were involved, directly or indirectly.

The entrepreneurial Brown brothers, James and Obadiah, were already successful merchants when they decided to diversify their holdings and invest in the booming slavery sector. In 1736, their first ship put Providence on the slave-trade map and opened up a new income stream for the Browns. Over the next couple of decades the family kept its slave trading local, avoiding the risks of the high seas. But in the late 1750s James's four sons, John, Nicholas, Joseph, and Moses, wishing to benefit from their age's biggest cash cow, plunged back in. They made money, but there were still risks, not the least of which was that the slave business was rapidly becoming a craze, like the dot-com boom. If you were looking for a quick buck and had no moral qualms, you wanted in on the action. Eventually, an oversupply of rum and an undersupply of potential slaves motivated the invisible hand of the marketplace to start slapping the business pretty hard, and it became increasingly difficult to, shall we say, make a killing buying and selling people. Pic-

---

* By 1764, there were about thirty distilleries in microscopic Rhode Island.

ture an enormous fleet of ships off the west coast of Africa—
more than two dozen from wee Rhode Island alone—trying to
avoid crashing into each other* as their agents onshore strug-
gled to make deals.

Finally, three of the four Brown brothers reevaluated their
investment priorities, assessed their risk tolerance, and reallo-
cated their resources to other divisions of the family firm—
their whale-oil candle works, for instance, and their iron
foundry. The fourth brother, John, redoubled his commitment
to the intercontinental slave import-export racket, becoming
an outspoken advocate for the practice. After brother Noah
had a come-to-Jesus moment/nervous breakdown and turned
against the business of human bondage, the two clashed often
and publicly.

Honoré de Balzac has been misquoted as saying that behind
every great fortune lies a great crime. These hyperbolic, inaccurately ascribed† words should be kept in mind as a preventive
against future embarrassment by every high-minded institution ready to exchange naming rights for big, fat donations.
Case in point: the College of Rhode Island. It was founded in
1764 and supported from the start by the Browns and others in
the local moneyed set (including the governor of the colony and
foundry partner of the Browns, **Stephen Hopkins**). The proxi-
mate cause of the name change from CRI to Brown U, in 1804,
was a gift from Nicholas Brown, Jr. (class of 1786), although it
was also surely a tip of the mortarboard to forty years of Brown
family philanthropy—philanthropy funded in large measure

---

* Like oversized, floating, dungeon-equipped bumper cars.

† Inaccurately ascribed by C. Wright Mills and Mario Puzo and the forgotten novelist
Samuel Merwin and the forgotten French writer Pierre Mille and some Brit politician
ridiculously named James Henry Yoxall and too many others to cram into a totally
unnecessary footnote.

by the family's super-non-PC predilection for abducting and enslaving Africans. As this fake tweet so eloquently states: BROWNS' SKEEVY BIZ DEALINGS ARE, OR SHOULD BE, A CONTINUING MORTIFICATION TO 21ST-CENTURY BROWN STUDENTS, PROFS, ADMINS, & GRADS!!!#SHAME.

# William F. Buckley, Jr.

*BA, Yale University*

Bill Buckley! "Patron saint" of conservatism, polysyllabic sesquipedalianist, and role model for every insufferable twit, genteel racist, and snot-nosed reactionary douchebag of the past sixty years!

Buckley graduated an Eli (with honors) in 1950. A year later the whole world learned, in *God and Man at Yale,* just how mad he was at his socialistic, atheistic professors (in the Religious Studies Department!). The book caused a stir. Some said Buckley's fervent Catholicism made him a less-than-ideal critic of the treatment of religion at the essentially Protestant university. But others were thrilled to discover a smart, young conservative voice, a voice that brought conservatism into the twentieth century by combining traditionalism with libertarianism (good luck with *that*) and anticommunism.

Presumably they were similarly thrilled when, in the August 24, 1957, issue of *National Review,* Buckley published the editorial "Why the South Must Prevail." In it, he wrote that until "long term equality could be achieved," segregation was necessary. "The central question that emerges…is whether the White community in the South is entitled to take such measures as are necessary to prevail, politically and culturally, in areas where it does not predominate numerically? The sobering answer is Yes — the White community is so entitled because, for the time being, it is the advanced race."

Sure, this came barely twelve years after the Allied defeat of Nazi Germany, whose doctrine of the "master race" had become (and remains) the very definition of evil. But look at the fancy language! Buckley's editorial is not even a denial of southern racism, but a defense of it:

> It is not easy, and it is unpleasant, to adduce statistics evidencing the median cultural superiority of White over Negro but it is a fact that obtrudes, one that cannot be hidden by ever-so-busy egalitarians and anthropologists. The question, as far as the White community is concerned, is whether the claims of civilization supersede those of universal suffrage.

But *is* it "unpleasant"? To disagree with those ever-so-busy egalitarians? Not really. There's more:

> NATIONAL REVIEW believes that the South's premises are correct. If the majority wills what is socially atavistic, then to thwart the majority may be, though undemocratic, enlightened. It is more important for any community, anywhere in the world, to affirm and live by civilized standards, than to bow to the demands of the numerical majority. Sometimes it becomes impossible to assert the will of a minority, in which case it must give way, and the society will regress; sometimes the numerical minority cannot prevail except by violence: then it must determine whether the prevalence of its will is worth the terrible price of violence.

(Tr.: If the Negroes are federally guaranteed the vote, they'll destroy civilization. The South must prevent this — by violence, if necessary, after first deciding whether it's worth it.)

To be sure, the South "must not exploit the fact of Negro backwardness to preserve the Negro as a servile class." Glad we got *that* straight. And, therefore,

> So long as it is merely asserting the right to impose superior mores for whatever period it takes to effect a genuine cultural equality between the races, and so long as it does so by humane and charitable means, the South is in step with civilization.

In other words, keep segregation, Jim Crow, "colored only" drinking fountains and swimming pools and lunch counters and neighborhoods and schools, and wait patiently as the white South gradually brings the Negroes and their "mores" up to speed. The beatings will continue until morale improves.

Buckley mitigated these views — or thought he did; or claimed he did — over time. He later said it was a mistake for *National Review* to have opposed the civil rights legislation of 1964–65, and that he grew to admire Martin Luther King, Jr. Still, as late as 2004 he was pleased to play footsie with vocabulary. "The point I made about white cultural supremacy was sociological," he told the *New York Times Magazine*. "The call for the 'advancement' of colored people presupposes they are behind," he said, perhaps never having heard of the American Association for the Advancement of Science. "Which they were, in 1958, by any standards of measurement." (Tr.: See? Even the NAACP thought Negroes were backward. And look at their name! They still do!)

Speaking of the advanced race, Buckley visited South Africa in 1962, courted and brought there by the Information Ministry, making Buckley what Ta-Nehisi Coates calls "a press agent for apartheid." Buckley wrote that apartheid "has evolved into a serious program designed to cope with a melodramatic dilemma on whose solution hangs, quite literally, the question of life or death for the white man in South Africa." As with desegregation in the South, so with apartheid: Buckley presents the problem as the solution.

But it would be a mistake to think of Buckley as merely the thinking man's racist. To his credit, he denounced Robert Welch and the John Birch Society, condemned anti-Semitism, and ran Whittaker Chambers's scathing takedown of Ayn Rand's *Atlas Shrugged*.

Then again, he was also the thinking man's defender of right-wing thugs and dictators. He supported the vile Spanish strongman (and *SNL* punch line) Francisco Franco, calling him "an authentic national hero." He cheered the coup that overthrew the democratically elected Chilean (Marxist) president Salvador Allende and brought to power central-casting dictator Augusto Pinochet. The Chilean government later revealed that during Pinochet's rule more than 3,000 people had been killed or "disappeared," as many as 40,000 political enemies were tortured, and 80,000 were imprisoned. But when Buckley interviewed Pinochet while it was happening and the *supremo* denied any involvement with all that, Buckley "was inclined to believe him." "Inclined" is right.

Is that all? Yes, except for when Orlando Letelier, a Chilean activist and exile in Washington, DC, was blown up by a car bomb, and Buckley and *National Review* conducted an ongoing campaign hinting or stating—falsely—that Letelier had been a Cuban or Soviet agent.

Oh, and there was that terribly unfortunate AIDS business in the 1980s, when Buckley recommended that "everyone detected with AIDS should be tattooed in the upper forearm, to protect common-needle users, and on the buttocks, to prevent the victimization of other homosexuals."

As for the rest—his self-parodying languor; his snobbery disguised as discrimination; his clotted, show-offy prose style that's influenced two generations of unreadably arch, nitwit "conservatives"; his enthusiastic support for right-wing kook Barry Goldwater and dithering actor-in-chief Reagan; his fondness for peanut butter and Bach and sailing—why bother? One of Yale's most famous graduates proclaimed he was "standing athwart History yelling Stop," when he was in fact obstructing progress, murmuring tautologies, and cosseting villains.

# George W. Bush

*BA, Yale University* ★ *MBA, Harvard University*

Let's pretend there's a parallel universe in which George W. Bush was born into a different family but possessed the character and intellect of the man we know. Yes, it's ridiculous, but c'mon, play along. We'll make his family white, middle class, suburban, two working parents, public school for the kids, the usual. Remember, our guy has the same character and mental horsepower as the real guy.

Here's the question: Does he go to Yale, followed by Harvard Business School? Does he, as a teenager, even have the curiosity to *think* about where to go to college? Does he register that some colleges are considered more desirable than others? Does he learn the names of those good colleges? Does he understand that he'd better work hard in high school if he wants to have a chance of getting into a good college?

You're thinking that if George W. Bush had been born into a regular middle-class family, he *wouldn't* necessarily have become a cocky, belligerent, bullying, lazy, spoiled little prick like the real guy, right? Oh, come on. It's a *Gedankenexperiment*.* Play along! But remember: if you tell us you can imagine him going to Yale, then to Harvard Business, then charming his way into the Air National Guard to avoid Vietnam, then making some crappy business deals that he miraculously profits from,

---

* A mental experiment, like the one with Schrödinger's cat, although in this case we have two different people who are at once the same person rather than one cat who is in two different states (alive/dead) at once.

then running a dirty campaign* and being elected governor of Texas, then running for president of the USA, we'll know you're lying.

No, the best imaginable outcome for our make-believe George Jr. (whose make-believe grandfather† was not a Yale graduate,‡ a wealthy banker, president of the United States Golf Association, or a senator from Connecticut, and whose make-believe father was not a Yale graduate,§ a congressman, an ambassador to the United Nations, chairman of the Republican National Committee, director of Central Intelligence, or president of the USA) would be something like day manager of a Wendy's. Or salesman at a Ford dealership. Or maybe owner of a small landscaping company. And at worst you'd have a guy who just barely graduates from high school, gets drafted, goes to Vietnam, and eight months later is shot by three guys in his platoon because they can't stand the sight of him.

George W. Bush — the real one, whose father was president, and whose mother, Barbara Pierce Bush, was a distant cousin of another president¶ — was accepted at Yale for one reason. It wasn't a meritocratic reason like terrific high-school grades, brilliant violin playing, a world-class squash game, or perfect SAT scores. No, he was accepted at Yale because of his last name, plain and simple. Whatever civilizing powers Yale may claim flew right past his antennae; after his graduation he was exactly the same smug, smirky, nasty, ignorant jackass he'd

---

* Highlighted by innuendos that his opponent was a lesbian. Hi there, Karl Rove!

† And make-believe grandfather's grandfather and make-believe grandfather's great-uncle.

‡ And member of hush-hush secret society Skull and Bones.

§ And member of hush-hush secret society Skull and Bones.

¶ Franklin Pierce, president no. 14, who supported slavery and drank himself to death.

been before he arrived for freshman orientation. And then we have Harvard Business School, which accepted him for one reason. Hint: It wasn't his mediocre grades at Yale. Or even his dazzling work as a Yale cheerleader.

Unfortunately for humanity, the real George W. did run for president. He attracted many voters who didn't know a thing about Yale but were thrilled to be voting for a presidential candidate who appeared to be as shit-kickin' ignorant as their own friends and relatives, not to mention themselves. Someone who'd be fun to have a drink with.*

Skipping over the 2000 election — we'll postpone that insanity for the **Al Gore, Joe Lieberman,** and **Ralph Nader** entries, among others — we shall now attempt to say a few words about his presidency without bursting into tears and ruining our computers.

On August 6, 2001, the president, vacationing at his "ranch" (where, like his fake-ranch-owning predecessor Ronald Reagan, he was often photographed "clearing brush") in Crawford, Texas,† received an intelligence briefing with the headline "Bin Laden Determined to Strike in US." Bush brushed off his CIA briefer, famously saying, "All right. You've covered your ass now." A few weeks later: 9/11. That catastrophe caused the Bush neocons (among them **Douglas Feith** and **Richard Perle**) to orgasm simultaneously as they envisioned their long-held fantasy — of invading Iraq and overthrowing Saddam Hussein — capable of being realized, even though there was zero relationship between the attack and Saddam Hussein.

George Senior had prudently decided not to march to Bagh-

---

* As a "dry drunk," W no longer imbibed, yet appeared to be in a permanent alcoholic stupor. This, apparently, appealed to these voters.

† To trick morons into mistaking him for a Texas cowpoke.

dad during *his* Gulf War. Now Junior saw a chance to prove he was more of a he-man/BMOC than his daddy could ever hope to be, so he was happy to get behind the neocon Iraq adventure, and to lie repeatedly* in order to coerce the American public into supporting him. Meantime, Osama bin Laden and the other top dogs of al-Qaeda were in remote Afghanistan ("The Graveyard of Empires"), laughing their asses off.

Bush's ignorance, multiplied by his oedipal problems, multiplied by his dependence on the mentally unsound and/or casually brutal posse surrounding him, multiplied by his unthinking religiosity, plus some constant (call it $T$ for Texas macho bullshit), yielded a great deal of spilled blood, damaged Americans and Iraqis, destroyed architecture, and ruined landscapes, not to mention the billions of dollars that were, and continue to be, vaporized. Let alone the creation of the conditions that undergird the birth of ISIL, ISIS, DAESH, the caliphate, THRUSH, SMERSH, the Borg, KAOS, or whatever the fuck you call it.

Mission accomplished, Junior.

---

* For instance, about the existence of WMDs. About the connection between Saddam and al-Qaeda. About Iraq's purchase of fissionable "yellowcake" uranium. About a peaceful aftermath and being "greeted as liberators." About the venture being paid for "by the oil." We could go on.

# John C. Calhoun

*BA, Yale University*

John C. Calhoun was a prominent American politician, states-man, and public intellectual during the first half of the nine-teenth century. Among other accomplishments, he was:

- Elected congressman and twice elected senator from his home state of South Carolina
- Appointed secretary of war by President James Monroe
- Twice elected vice president, serving under John Quincy Adams and Andrew Jackson
- Appointed secretary of state by President John Tyler
- A brilliant orator who was known as the Cast-Iron Man for his unbendable convictions

Impressive, even for a class of 1804 Phi Beta Kappa Yale gradu-ate. Except for one problem.

The man loved slavery.

Adored it. Wanted to *marry* it. Thought it was the bee's knees. Waxed eloquent about it. And in his waxings, unlike the many apologists for slavery who argued that it was a "necessary evil," Calhoun proclaimed it a "positive good." Slavery, to this gentle-man, reflected the God-given superiority of the white race and conferred benefits on everyone, including the slaves themselves. And isn't it great when that happens? When, while getting rich oppressing others, you're not only serving the Almighty but actually doing good for the oppressed? You bet it is.

Still—and how is this even fair?—there are pesky do-gooders in every society. As antislavery sentiments bloomed in the North, Calhoun's rhetoric turned from moral and religious to calculatedly political, invoking "states' rights" and the concept of "nullification," in which a state can—and must!—overrule the federal government when it starts getting too uppity. And, don't you know, we hear these terms from Republicans—mostly from the South, but not exclusively—to this very day. Isn't it funny, how little some things change over time?

Although Calhoun, who died in 1850, did not live to witness the logical conclusion of his prodigious speechifying, he more than anyone else could be said to be the guy who started the Civil War. Too much? Okay. Then let it be said that he was one of slavery's most eloquent, rigid, and self-righteous defenders. Better?

Over the course of Yale's first two centuries, Calhoun was the only graduate to be elected to a superprestigious position in the US government. Ergo, Yale is, or at least was, proud of its association with him and is, or was, rife with commemorative Calhounabilia, including a statue perched, alongside statues of other notable graduates, on the Gothic gingerbread of Harkness Tower; a residence called Calhoun College; and, within this residence, a stained-glass depiction of the man himself, posing with a kneeling, shackled, and no doubt grateful black man.

Alas (for those sympathetic to slavery, states' rights, and Calhoun—we know you're out there), it eventually dawned on a significant number of students, faculty, and Yale administrators that glorifying not just "a racist," but a proud-talking,

Bible-thumping, opposite-of-apologetic racist, might strike some as being slightly offensive. (By "some" we mean blacks, whites, Asians, Latinos, men, women, civilized persons, and humans in general.) Such a policy might arguably not be in the school's best interest. So in 1992 Yale slapped up a poster in Calhoun College acknowledging the controversial nature of the dorm's eponym.

But how to address the problematic nature of the stained-glass masterpiece depicting Calhoun's dominion over and ownership of a slave? Easy: Yale brought in an artisan to remove the slave from the artwork. Now, if the Communist Party of the Soviet Union had done something like that to a painting of Stalin — say, removed from a group portrait the faces of men he was discovered to have brutally murdered, but kept the rest — we would have tsked and tutted and shaken our heads in appalled moral superiority. Yale, though, went about its business, perhaps resisting the urge to replace the slave with a sign reading YOUR AD HERE.*

Of course this did not settle the issue.

There are those who want to cleanse Yale of all overt associations with John C. Calhoun, to toss him down the memory hole, as it were. But whitewashing the past is not the way it's done — or, at least, should be done — by an institution dedicated to, among other things, researching, teaching, and attempting to understand history.

Here's our suggestion: Rename the dorms, then scoop up the artifacts associated with *all* the honored Yalie miscreants (there are plenty of them; we've pointed out some of them right here in this book), and deposit them in their own little museum.

---

* What Yale actually did was replace the slave with panels representing what appears to be an overcast sky — which is at Calhoun's feet and below the cupola of the US Capitol. Once a racist stained-glass window, now a work of surrealist art!

Create an Ivy Hall of Shame, as it were. Don't worry about funding it; some rich graduates destined to be enshrined therein will surely pay for it as long as their names are spelled correctly and they have approval of their portraits and/or busts. Let it be a place of study, contemplation, and learning, of service to anyone looking to counteract the delusional belief that the mere act of graduating from such an establishment necessarily places one on the right side of history.

# Robert Cantor

*BA, University of Pennsylvania ★ MA, University of Pennsylvania ★ PhD Candidate, University of Pennsylvania*

Robert Cantor lived alone in an apartment in Philadelphia. He was, his neighbors said, as they so often do in cases like this, a quiet man who never spoke with anyone. He'd received his BA and MA in math from Penn and was working on his PhD thesis under Dr. Walter Koppelman. According to another professor in the department, Cantor was under severe strain. It had been eight years since he'd earned his master's, which suggests a possible reason for that severe strain.

On February 11, 1970, Cantor walked into a math seminar attended by about twenty-five students and faculty members and fired a number of shots from a .45-caliber automatic at Dr. Koppelman and another faculty member. He then stepped outside and killed himself with one shot to the head.

The other faculty member recovered quickly, but Dr. Koppelman died in a hospital fifteen days later. Koppelman was born in Vienna in 1929. His parents fled Austria and brought him to New York when he was eleven. He was a music and mathematics genius who escaped the Nazis only to have his life blasted out of him, at age forty, by a thesis-crazed Ivy League graduate student.

We're not sure whether math drives people crazy, or crazy people are attracted to math.* You make the call.

---

\* See **Ted Kaczynski**.

# Dr. Ben Carson

*BA, Yale University*

Until Ben Carson shambled into the (secular) national consciousness, the phrase "brain surgeon" was a commonly used stand-in for "person of high intelligence," who "knows a lot about many things, including brain surgery," as in "**George W. Bush** is no brain surgeon." Thanks to his presidential bid, in Ben Carson we encountered — perhaps for the first time — a brain surgeon who knows nothing about anything *except* brain surgery. Post-Carson, the phrase will most likely be retired, its work to be carried on by "rocket scientist," "Einstein," and, possibly, "Elon Musk."

Carson had a nasty childhood: black, Detroit, dirt poor, single mother, the whole underclass enchilada. But he was driven. He worked hard enough in school to end up at Yale. He did well enough there to go on to medical school at the University of Michigan, followed by a neurosurgery residency at Johns Hopkins. At the tender age of thirty-three he was named director of pediatric surgery at Hopkins. He was reputedly brilliant, published many papers, and, among a multitude of medical accomplishments, successfully separated a pair of conjoined twins. True, one suffered brain damage and the other died. But you can't win every battle. All told, it's a nearly mythological American success story.

However.

In 2004 Carson formed an endorser-style relationship with Mannatech, a shady nutritional-supplement firm that wrapped

itself in Christian mumbo-jumbo while a) including the magic syllable "tech" in its name, and b) claiming its products cured cancer and autism. Because why stop with mere cancer?

In 2013 he retired from medicine, soon thereafter declaring himself a 2016 Republican presidential candidate. He had already published several Christian-themed books of inspirational uplift, including an autobiography, a book "based on" the autobiography, a book for kids based on the autobiography, and no fewer than three "whither America?" tomes entitled *America the Beautiful: Rediscovering What Made This Nation Great; One Nation: What We Can All Do to Save America's Future;* and *A More Perfect Union: What We the People Can Do to Reclaim Our Constitutional Liberties.* And, in case there was anyone left who didn't get the message, there was *What I Believe: A Collection of My Syndicated Columns.*

Carson was therefore already famous and adored by the right-wing fundamentalists who wield so much power in the UFC® mud-wrestling lie-a-thon we call "the Republican primaries." So why not run for president? Who cares—indeed, who will notice—if you know nothing of other countries, little about recent history, and less than nothing about how our government works? Why *shouldn't* you get donors to fund your toddling around America, fielding softball questions you can't answer, and promoting your books?

During Carson's campaign, the rest of nonkook America (to the extent that there is any) met a pleasant-looking, spookily calm, eerily soft-spoken gent whose mild demeanor contrasted so nicely with the bellicose snarling of his campaign rivals. And

Carson's utterances (often said with half-closed eyes, as though delivered by a man in a jolly, cocktail-party hypnotist's trance) had an effect.

The effect was to leave his audience gasping with incredulity. Here was a scientist who indicated that he rejected the scientific method; a master of materialist medicine (you can't get more materialist than cracking open skulls and cutting out pieces of brains) who accepted fundamentalist, antimaterialist Christian dogma; and an Ivy League graduate who called evolution a "myth" encouraged by you-know-who. (Guess. Guess who. You'll never guess. That's right: Satan himself. "I personally believe that this theory that Darwin came up with was something that was encouraged by the Adversary.")

Carson, a literal brain surgeon who made a career correcting damage to the human organism, thinks there aren't enough guns in circulation. Carson, a literal African American, likens anything he doesn't embrace either to slavery or the Nazis. During his campaign the good doctor, in his whispery way, told us that he:

- Wants to outlaw all abortions
- Wants to get rid of Medicare
- Thinks we should not allow a Muslim to be president
- Does not believe in the concept of war crimes
- Believes being gay is a choice (for reasons too dumb to detail even here)
- Believes God created the universe 6,000 years ago
- Calls the Big Bang a "fairy tale"
- Rejects the scientific consensus on climate change
- Thinks women who get abortions are like slave owners
- Thinks Obamacare is the worst thing to happen to America since slavery

- Advocates punishing colleges that allow too much liberal speech
- Believes there's a good chance that anarchy will soon reign and Obama will declare martial law and call off the 2016 election. (Remember, this was said during the 2016 presidential campaign.)
- Thinks Obama's natty way of dressing proves he's a psychopath
- Believes advanced-placement history classes encourage young people to join ISIS
- Thinks that if German Jews had been packing heat there would have been no Holocaust*
- Thinks Hamas is pronounced "hummus"
- Never was involved with Mannatech, despite copious evidence to the contrary
- Believes America is "very much like Nazi Germany. And I know you're not supposed to say 'Nazi Germany,' but I don't care about political correctness. You know, you had a government using its tools to intimidate the population. We now live in a society where people are afraid to say what they actually believe."

And more. Far too much more.

In the medical community it is well understood that it doesn't take an intellectual giant to be a surgeon—just good training, steady nerves, excellent hand-eye coordination, and a mammoth ego. The hospital floor wisdom is, "Surgeons know nothing and do everything; internists know everything and do nothing; and psychiatrists know nothing and do nothing."

---

* Did he get this from **Dr. Keith Ablow**? Or vice versa? Or is it just that muddled minds think alike?

Clearly, Dr. Ben Carson is living proof of the first clause: he is indeed an accomplished surgeon, and he indeed seems to know nothing. Fine. What's disturbing — and somewhat monstrous — is that this quietly murmuring source of reactionary nonsense, brute ignorance, and outright lies is a graduate of *Yale*.

Who thought he should be president!*

---

* All of which means he was a brilliant choice for **Donald Trump**'s cabinet.

# Andrew W. W. Caspersen

*BA, Princeton University ★ JD, Harvard University*

If you're wondering how to know whether you're leading a privileged life, here are some telltale signs:

- Your father is a graduate of Harvard Law School. As are your three older brothers. As are you.
- Your family name is affixed to the façade of the student center at Harvard Law School.
- Your family name is Caspersen.

Check, check, and check. Congratulations, Mr. Andrew Caspersen.

Andrew's father, Finn, who graduated from Brown before going to Harvard Law, was the chairman and CEO of the Beneficial Corporation.* It was surely beneficial to him when the company sold for $8.6 billion in 1998. In the years following the sale, it was not unheard-of for tabloids and financial rags to refer to Finn as a "billionaire." He was, without question, rich, with "seaside estates" in Rhode Island and Florida, and a strong interest in showy philanthropy. In addition to the $30 million† that bought the name of the student center and other tangible items at Harvard Law, he endowed two professorships. And

---

* Consumer finance. Which Finn's father ran before Finn did.

† At least that's the number Finn claimed and the media repeated. Except for *Vanity Fair,* which pegs the gift at a measly $1.5 million.

supported the United States Equestrian Team. And various rowing programs. Not to mention the Caspersen School of Graduate Studies at Drew University. And much more!

Yes, it's an inspiring American story about benefits and corporations — but, as so many such stories do, this one now takes a strange and sad turn.

Weak and depressed from a long battle with kidney cancer, Finn shot himself in the head in 2009. Or maybe he didn't have cancer. Maybe that just became the family line to sidestep the allegation that he was insolvent and under investigation by the IRS for the millions of dollars in taxes he owed. (Ultimately, the government dropped the case against Finn's estate.)

Oh but, dearly beloved, we are gathered here today to discuss Finn's youngest son. Andrew, like his brothers — all three of whom work for banks or investment firms — followed the money: after Harvard Law, he took a job with a private-equity firm, rose through the ranks, and made a lot of money. In 2013 he started at another firm and continued making a lot of money.*

And then things went all bizarro for Andrew Caspersen. In late 2014, he started soliciting investors for a deal he claimed would return 15 percent a year with minimal risk.† With his impeccable credentials, connections, pedigree, personal and family wealth, wardrobe, manner of speaking, and cut of jib, he collected...well, as of this writing no one seems to know exactly how much he collected. It's said to be at least $40 million and could be considerably more. Which would have been perfectly

---

* His 2015 salary was reportedly $3.68 million. That's $70,769 a week, or $14,154 a day (assuming five-day workweeks), or $1,769 an hour (eight-hour workdays). That's $29.48 a minute (sixty-minute hours), which doesn't sound like such a big deal. Hey, one of us once *spent* that much on Amazon.com *in less than a minute!*

† His pitch probably didn't include the line "Why, you couldn't have done better with Bernie Madoff himself!" Meanwhile, you ask, "Is 15 percent good?" Dude. (May we call you dude?) The average investor return for 2014 was a little over 4 percent.

wonderful if the money had been going where he said it was going. But it wasn't.

There was no "deal." It was, in fact, a "fraud."

Caspersen took money from wherever he could get it—old Princeton friends, a charity run by a hedge-fund billionaire, his brothers, even his actual biological *mother.* Then, after passing it through a shell corporation he'd set up, he gambled it away on high-risk short-term stock options. Unfortunately for him and his unwitting investors, he was an extremely bad stock-options gambler. By the end of his bender, all but $40,000* of the money he'd collected was gone.

On March 26, 2016, on the way home from a Florida vacation, Andrew Caspersen was arrested at LaGuardia Airport, on federal securities and wire-fraud charges, in front of his wife and two young children. He was released on a $5 million bond—secured by his $1.1 million house in Bronxville, his $2.3 million Manhattan co-op,† and guarantees from his wife and one of his brothers.‡ As a condition of his release, he had to be treated for alcohol abuse and, for obvious reasons, undergo psychiatric evaluation. Needless to say, he was summarily axed from the job in the financial-services sector that had been paying him nearly fifty cents a second.

Andrew Caspersen has had a lot of bad news over the past several years, including learning of, and having to come to terms with, his inadequacy as a Ponzi schemer.

The good news for him is that, although he faced a maxi-

---

* That's only 2.83 days of earnings at his aforementioned job.

† A mere twenty miles away from the Bronxville residence. Why? Why?

‡ The bail terms were later changed to $1 million cash, plus a $5 million bond secured by three people, plus the Bronxville house, minus the Manhattan co-op. You can't put up a Manhattan co-op as bond. We could have told them that—not from personal experience, mind you. From the miracle of *knowledge.*

mum sentence of up to forty years in prison, he'll end up doing a mere four. Having the resources to know, hire, and pay for an excellent attorney is one of the privileges of privilege.

And while it's unlikely that he'll ever work in Big Money again, and will no doubt be barred from practicing law, Andrew Caspersen will always have the comfort of knowing that there's a building with his surname on it at ultraprestigious Harvard Law School.

# Benjamin Church

*BA, Harvard University*

He's been called America's first traitor* and America's worst traitor. Why? First, because, well, he was first; worst, because if he'd done his job a little better there might be no United States of America.

Born in 1734 to a prominent New England family, Benjamin Church studied medicine† at Harvard, graduating in 1754.‡ He traveled to England to continue his studies, made an English lady his wife, and returned to Boston to practice medicine. He quickly earned a reputation as an excellent physician, surgeon, and apothecary. He also earned a reputation as an author of patriotic — prorevolutionary — orations and poems as the Revolutionary War approached.§ He was on chummy terms with John Adams, Samuel Adams, Paul Revere, and, of course, John Hancock. He was the first doctor to treat the injured at the Boston Massacre of 1770. He was elected to the Massachusetts Provisional Congress after the Boston Tea Party. He was, before the country existed, the equivalent of the first surgeon general of the United States.

---

* Trouncing the infamous Benedict Arnold by five years.

† As an undergrad. There was no graduate medical school until 1782, and Church was dead by then, so it was out of the question.

‡ Alongside his classmate the signature artist John Hancock.

§ He was first acclaimed as a poet for two 1760 works celebrating the coronation of King George III, who, in the 1770s, was the top bad guy of the American Revolution. If Church's peers had been paying attention, they might have been able to prevent his treacherous doings later.

All in all, an outstanding collection of revolutionary credentials. But he had a fatal flaw: a lust for luxury, starting with an
expensive summer place and a house in a ritzy part of Boston.
Although he was spending his way into deep financial doo-doo,
he always seemed to have a large supply of fresh British guin-
eas.* Paul Revere and other peers didn't necessarily know about
the money problems and the British gold, but they grew suspicious when Dr. Church visited the home of General Thomas
Gage, commander in chief of the British forces in North America. When the details of a secret meeting of revolutionaries were
leaked to Americans loyal to the king, Revere was convinced
that Church was the snitch.

The end for Church arrived with a serving of sordid-sauce.†
He gave his pregnant mistress, an off-duty prostitute named
Mary Wenwood, a coded letter to take to a British officer. She,
a master of the bad decision, brought in her ex-husband for
assistance. The sight of a letter written in mysterious code
freaked him out, and he turned it in to the rebel authorities. It
quickly found its way to General George Washington himself,
who had it deciphered,‡ saw that it contained secrets meant to
help the British—like the amount of gunpowder his army had
stockpiled—and brought in Wenwood for questioning. She, of
course, implicated the priapic, upwardly mobile Dr. Church.

Church did not deny that he was the author of the treasonous document. He did, however, claim that it wasn't treasonous.
Its purpose, he said, was to mislead his British contacts into
thinking Washington's army was so strong and well provisioned

---

* Gold coins, not feathered creatures of the class *Aves*, order *Galliformes,* family *Numi-didae.* A guinea, if we remember our Sherlock Holmes aright, was worth a pound and a shilling.

† We're pretending we lifted this sentence from the pages of the *Colonial Enquirer.*

‡ Clearly, this was not a da Vinci–level code job.

that it couldn't be defeated, forcing the redcoats to give up and go home. Or something like that. He was applauded for his creativity, charged with treason, convicted, and sentenced to life in prison without the use of pen, ink, or paper.

John Adams was appalled by his friend's betrayal, fearing it could undermine the revolution. But it did not. The Americans, which is what we now call them,* won! In a 1778 doctor-for-doctor swap, the Americans agreed to exchange Dr. Church for Dr. James McHenry, a surgeon the British were holding. Church boarded a sloop for Martinique, the first leg of his journey to England, but the ship, with its passengers and crew, was lost at sea. He never got to entertain English friends with his poems or tales of derring-do and skullduggery during the American Revolution, set up an apothecary shop, or advise undergraduates looking to spend a semester at Harvard, if they had that back then, which they didn't.

Mrs. Church and the Church children escaped to England, destitute; a mob torched their fancy house in Boston. Her only consolation was the pension the British government gave her as the wife of a fallen spy.

---

* Because "United Statesians" is uberclunky.

# Bill Clinton

*JD, Yale University*

No, we're not going to regale you with the list of fake infractions, crimes, murders, genocides, and so on that the Republicans have been inventing* about Bill Clinton since he was the governor of Arkansas. And if you're looking for an attack from the left flank, get yourself a copy of Thomas Frank's *Listen, Liberal*† and knock yourself out. Instead, we're going to focus our attention on a certain, shall we say, *insufficiency* that led to horrific unintended consequences with reverberations that just won't quit.

Like many highly educated, highly ambitious people of high attainment, Clinton has, or at least had, a propensity to behave as if he were invisible. You'd think famous people would understand that the opposite is the case, i.e., that part of the deal they make with the devil requires that their possessing a private life is a thing of the past. But not all of them do.

It's probably diagnosable as a form of narcissistic personality disorder when you, a famous person, engage in any type of

---

* Because it's beneath us. And you. And we'll deal with some of them in our entry on **Kenneth Starr**.

† In which Clinton and many other Ivy-educated liberal politicians are accused of willfully abandoning the traditional working-class base of the Democratic Party in favor of rich, "well-graduated" technocrats just like themselves.

sexual activity with a near stranger and assume that the near stranger will, afterward, go on his or her way and not mention to anyone that he or she recently had sex with a famous person simply because you said, "Oh, by the way, don't tell anyone we did this." It's even worse if the sexual activity was not consensual, as certain women have alleged — not necessarily convincingly — about Clinton. It was bad enough that Clinton was involved in, or was alleged to have been involved in, a few of these incidents* while he was governor. It is unforgivable that he had any while he was president. If you can't keep it zipped for four years, or even eight years,† perhaps you should be seeking a different line of work.

It was inevitable that Clinton's White House dalliance with Monica Lewinsky would eventually be revealed to the world at large.‡ That led to the egregious GOP impeachment stampede (led by a cadre of affair-having hypocrites), which contributed to the Democrats' loss of the next presidential contest§ and the "election" of **George W. Bush**, followed by an entirely unnecessary and ongoing pile of corpses in Iraq, Afghanistan — you get our drift. It had to be the worst series-of-unintended-consequences-to-follow-a-few-blow-jobs *ever.*

We hope you enjoyed them, Mr. President.

---

* There were enough of them to require an epithet. They were termed "bimbo eruptions" by Clinton advisor Betsy Wright.

† True, that's easy for us to say. We probably couldn't keep it zipped for eight *days,* with all that available action. But that's why we're not president.

‡ Name a twenty-four-year-old who wouldn't mention to *someone* that she was diddling the president of the United States of America. We'll wait. See? You can't do it.

§ See our entry on **Al Gore**, for instance.

# Morris Cohen

*MA, Columbia University*

**Tr**

It was the classic boy-meets-girl, boy-recruits-girl-to-be-Soviet-spy, boy-marries-girl, boy-and-girl-flee-to-Soviet-Union, boy-and-girl-go-undercover-to-England-as-antiquarian-book-dealers-are-arrested-serve-time-in-jail-and-eventually-live-happily-ever-after-in-Moscow story.

Unlike most first-generation Americans whose parents escaped the nightmare of Eastern Europe in the early days of the twentieth century, Morris Cohen did not grow up to become a rah-rah all-American boy. Cohen, born in the Bronx in 1910, became what he might well have become had his parents stayed put in Ukraine (his father) and/or Lithuania* (his mother): a communist. And not just a theoretical, after-school-commie-club kind of communist. After graduating from Mississippi State College† with a bachelor's degree in English, he joined the American Communist Party. Soon thereafter he shipped out to fight with the lefty Abraham Lincoln Brigade in the Spanish Civil War, where he took a bullet for the cause. During his recuperation, Soviet intelligence recruited him to spy on the USA.

In 1939 he returned the favor by recruiting another first-generation American and CPUSA member, Lona Petka (born of

---

* Ukraine and Lithuania are what we call these places today. We'd tell you what they were called back then but we know you couldn't care less. Why don't you just think of them as "Russia" and let us continue with the story? Thank you.

† Today's Mississippi State University. Why Mississippi? We have no idea. It makes as little sense to us as it does to you.

Polish Catholic parents), into the exciting world of espionage. With so much in common, the two married in 1941. Morris was soon drafted into the US Army and served in the Quartermaster Corps in Europe for three years; Lona honed her tradecraft stateside. As soon as Morris returned, the two of them got back together, living and loving and spying. Their finest hour came when they slipped Moscow blueprints of the first atomic bomb twelve days before it was tested in New Mexico. Stalin put his people to work on a knockoff posthaste.

For some reason — perhaps to have something to "fall back on" if the spying business didn't pan out, or perhaps as a cover — Morris Cohen entered Columbia University Teachers College in 1946. He got his MA in 1947, worked as a student teacher for a year at Benjamin Franklin High School in East Harlem, and received his license to teach the following year. It's not clear that he ever had time to use that license, since in 1950 the Cohens, learning that they were about to be arrested, fled to Moscow by way of Mexico. Fun times!

Fast-forward to 1954, when Morris and Lona, now carrying New Zealand passports in the names of Peter and Helen Kroger, set up shop as antiquarian book dealers in a cute house in suburban Ruislip, West London.* (By "cute" we mean "bristling with state-of-the-art spy equipment.") This adventure, dubbed the Portland Spy Ring, specialized in procuring info about the Royal Navy's submarine program. The operation lasted until early 1961, when the happy couple was busted by Special Branch detectives. In the house the coppers found photographic materials, message-coding pads, phony passports, large sums of

---

* A Bronx accent, and whatever accent Lona had, are nothing like a New Zealand accent. Did Moscow train them to speak like New Zealanders to trick the accent-astute Brits? Some reports say they posed as Canadians, which would have been easier for them to mimic, eh?

money, and a powerful radio transceiver (which took nine days of intense searching to unearth). More radio equipment turned up years later when the house was renovated.

Lona was sentenced to twenty years, Morris to twenty-five. They were out in eight, exchanged for an Englishman who was in prison in the Soviet Union for spreading anticommunist propaganda—which doesn't seem nearly as exciting as being a spy with all that cool equipment, passports, and cash, plus "ferrets," "baby-sitters," "lamplighters," "angels," "leash-dogs," and "pavement artists."*

The lovebirds lived out their days in a pleasant KGB-supplied dacha outside Moscow, refusing contact with their families and with decadent Western media (which is to say all Western media). Despite Morris's apparent thirst for education, he is said to have refused to learn Russian; perhaps it was too "old country" for him. He is also said to have eventually grown weary of the dullness of the totalitarian lifestyle—to the extent that a totalitarian society *has* a lifestyle. We'd like to think he occasionally wondered how things might have turned out if, after the war, he had allowed himself to outgrow his fatuous ideological purity, left behind the espionage racket, and gone back to teaching school in Harlem.

---

* Nifty spy lingo from John le Carré. Isn't it great? Who cares if it's authentic.

# Roy Cohn

*BA, Columbia University ★ LLD, Columbia University*

Something Cohn had, Donald liked.

> — SUSAN BELL, ROY COHN'S LONGTIME
> SECRETARY, NOTING THE AFFINITY BETWEEN
> HER BOSS AND **DONALD TRUMP**

Al Cohn was a mover and shaker in the Democratic Party, an assistant district attorney in the Bronx, and a justice of the

New York Supreme Court. Al Cohn's son, Roy, born into New York's legal aristocracy in 1927, also grew up to be a lawyer—a notoriously slimy one as well as an all-around douchebag.

He was a whiz kid who graduated from Columbia Law School at twenty and had to wait until he turned twenty-one to be admitted to the New York bar. The day he got his law license he started his first job—abetted by his father's connections—in the office of the US Attorney in Manhattan. He quickly made a name for himself as a foaming-at-the-mouth anticommunist, climaxing with his successful prosecution of Julius and Ethel Rosenberg for espionage in 1951. He proudly claimed responsibility for talking the judge into giving them the death penalty, even though such conversations between a prosecutor and the bench are not—what's the word?—oh, right: *legal*.

His anticommie crusade brought him to the attention of another closeted homosexual — have we mentioned that Roy Cohn was a closeted homosexual? — named J. Edgar Hoover, founding director of the FBI. Hoover tipped another Washington gargoyle, Senator Joseph McCarthy, that Cohn would make a fine chief counsel in the senator's own red-baiting witch-hunt with the Senate's Permanent Subcommittee on Investigations. One advantage Cohn had over the other leading candidate, Robert F. Kennedy,* was that Cohn was Jewish; appointing him would undermine the accusation that McCarthy's animus against communists was really an attack on Jews. (As Cohn himself said, "Not all Jews are communists, but most communists are Jews." See **Morris Cohen** for an example of one Jew who was, indeed, a communist.) And so the rapacious young Cohn teamed up with the crazed, dull-witted, alcoholic senator from Wisconsin to pursue commies.

Cohn and McCarthy would do anything to draw attention to their cause. A highly effective tactic was to fulminate about the threat of homosexuals in the government, the idea being that homosexuals were both communist sympathizers and highly susceptible to blackmail by communist agents seeking inside information. (Who, we ask you, would be more aware of the potential for, and potency of, blackmail than two closet cases and a drunk?) McCarthy, Cohn, and J. Edgar were ultimately responsible for the resignation or firing of hundreds of gay men from the State Department alone. In 1953, the wave of gayphobic hysteria† had swelled to the point where nice old President Dwight Eisenhower felt compelled to sign an

---

* Who was brought on as assistant counsel and hated Cohn for the rest of his life.

† Dubbed the Lavender Scare. You could look it up.

executive order banning homosexuals from the government altogether.*

Cohn's last hurrah with McCarthy was the Army-McCarthy hearings, initiated mainly by Cohn's attempt to force the US Army to give special treatment to a friend of his† who had been drafted; the army pushed back; McCarthy's committee stepped in to adjudicate; the hearings were televised; and the entire nation learned that Roy Cohn and Joe McCarthy were assholes. After the hearings Cohn left government "service" and went into private practice and a heavy nightlife schedule in New York.‡

Through his family connections, Cohn joined a reputable law firm. Within a dozen years, according to Robert Sherrill in *The Nation,* it was known as "the law firm that bought off judges, suborned witnesses and won cases through trickery and political pressure." Sometimes he'd demand cash from a client to bribe a judge and keep the money for himself. Or take a client's money, then do nothing to represent the client. Or let one client go to jail in order to get a client he liked better off the hook. Witness tampering? Check. Leaking confidential client information to the press to make himself look good? Check. Leaving a trail of unpaid bills?§ Ditto.

His law clients included mafiosi, nightclub proprietors, the Roman Catholic Archdiocese, and a young real estate heir from the outer boroughs named **Donald Trump,** to whom he became a mentor. An example of how Cohn and his "always

---

* Guess when this was overturned. No, you're wrong. It was overturned in 1995, when President Bill Clinton replaced it with the "Don't Ask, Don't Tell" policy that cleared the way for gay men and women to enter the military.

† Fellow commie hunter David Schine. Long story.

‡ McCarthy, meantime, focused on drinking himself to death.

§ Although he always promptly paid the homosexual prostitutes he hired.

attack, never apologize" philosophy — as well as his unrestrained disregard for the truth — rubbed off on Trump: in the early 1970s, when a far-reaching consent decree forced the Trump Organization to stop discriminating against blacks, Trump issued a Cohn-inspired press release proclaiming a sweeping victory over the Justice Department. Now that we think about it, the unapologetic, proudly mendacious stance of Roy Cohn could well have inspired the Republican Party *en masse* to take the murky path that left it, decades later, saddled with none other than Donald Trump (who also leaves a trail of unpaid bills) as its presidential candidate.* But enough of him. Back to the man of the hour, or at least of the chapter.

Columbia-educated Cohn ridiculed Harvard Law graduates for their old-fashioned adherence to legal and ethical norms.

Democrat Cohn made his name with Republican McCarthy and advised the administrations of Nixon and Reagan.

Jewish Cohn often referred to other Jews as "kikes."

Homosexual Cohn called gays "fags" and campaigned publicly against tolerance and in favor of legal sanctions.

In 1986 he was finally disbarred for, among other crimes, taking the hand of a rich, comatose former client, wrapping it around a pen, and scratching a signature on a codicil declaring Cohn to be a beneficiary.

Six weeks after his disbarment Cohn — one of the most truly repellent people in modern US history and a monster's monster — died of AIDS complications.

He never stopped denying he was gay.

---

* Which for some reason reminds us that Cohn joined the batshit right-wing John Birch Society in the 1960s.

# Ann Coulter

*BA, Cornell University*

But seriously: What *is* Ann Coulter?

Once, perhaps, she was the sex symbol of nasty conservative adolescents. It's nothing to be proud of, but it's a living. By  now they've abandoned her for the sexy-librarian allure of S. E. ("Sippy") Cupp or the gun-nut Annie Oakley posturings of Dana Loesch. Mind you, there's nothing wrong with a middle-aged woman resembling Saruman the White.* But you lose the teenagers. So now what? How does Ann Coulter fit into today's politico-infotainment ecology?

Is she a pundit? Please. If Ann Coulter is a pundit, then Ted Nugent is (former UN Secretary General) Ban Ki Moon. A pundit says things that, even if you disagree with them, are at least somewhat plausible. Whereas, about the 9/11 terrorists, Coulter said, "We should invade their countries, kill their leaders, and convert them to Christianity." Pause for a moment and imagine how that would go.

A journalist? I.e., a person dedicated to discovering and disseminating the truth? *Ha ha,* you slay us.

A "personality"? Like who—Ryan Seacrest? Try again.

Not even a "performance artist," which is the catchall term

---

* Power-crazed *Lord of the Rings* villain portrayed by Christopher Lee. You knew that, of course.

for anyone who does almost anything weird or repellent in public, on purpose.

No, the best Coulter's defenders can do, when explaining her toxic mix of reactionary commentary, rampant lying, and outright bigotry, is to call her a "humorist." It's all they've got. Never mind that to do so is to slander actual humorists from sea to shining sea.

If Ann Coulter, of fancy New Canaan, Connecticut, and $60,000-plus-per-annum (current retail) Cornell University, is a humorist, then it's a pity she never got the memo that humor—genuine humor, the kind that makes actual people actually laugh—aims at the powerful. In the parlance of many comedians (and humorists), humor must "punch *up*." It mocks the rich, the privileged, the smugly-in-control. Whereas Coulter, in sharp contrast, exclusively punches down. (To a disabled Vietnam vet: "People like you caused us to lose that war.") If only there were an everyday word for such a person! Oh, but wait. There is. It's "bully." And when she's not amusing herself and her sniggering gang of admirers by comforting the comfortable and afflicting the afflicted, she spends her time falsifying history and sneering at straw men she makes up and then calls "liberals." There's an everyday word for that, too.

Coulter is no more a humorist than Kermit the Frog is an amphibian. Rather, she's a soulless opportunist who realized long ago that there was a buck to be made (especially if you were female) funneling venomous scraps of hatred from the darkest, most squalid depths of the "conservative" id to the mouth-breathers of the right. To justify such dreck, to make it acceptable to polite society, Coulter and her enablers (her publishers, the shows that welcome her as a guest, networks that give her airtime) pretend she is a humorist. And by "pretend" we mean that every time she is accused of racism, anti-Semitism, or any other sort of "provocative" bigotry, she and/or her enablers blithely say, "Hey, it's *funny*. Don't you have a sense of humor?"

Molly Ivins got this right years ago:

> There are two kinds of humor. One kind that makes us chuckle about our foibles and our shared humanity — like what Garrison Keillor does. The other kind holds people up to public contempt and ridicule — that's what I do. Satire is traditionally the weapon of the powerless against the powerful. I only aim at the powerful. When satire is aimed at the powerless, it is not only cruel — it's vulgar.

In fact, nothing Ann Coulter has said or written can actually be said to constitute humor, with the sole exception of this hilarious one-liner: "Christianity fuels everything I write."

Ann Coulter as a sincere disciple of Jesus: now *that's* funny. (Shame on you, Cornell.)

# Ted Cruz

*BA, Princeton University* ★ *JD, Harvard University*

As solicitor general of Texas, Ted Cruz defended the state's ban*
on the sale of sex toys, or, as he called them, "obscene devices."
The government, according to his brief to the US Fifth Circuit
Court of Appeals, should have "police powers" to discourage
"prurient interest in sexual gratification"; the use of sex toys, in
Cruz's feverish mind, is like "hiring a willing
prostitute or engaging in consensual bigamy."
Lest you believe you have the right to do what
you want with yourself in the privacy of your
privacy, Cruz will have you know that "there is
no substantive-due-process right to stimulate
one's genitals for non-medical purposes unrelated to procreation or outside of an interper-
sonal relationship."†

Thus went his argument as a Texas politician. But where did he stand on the subject
when he was a Princeton undergrad? Cruz's
freshman-year roommate, the screenwriter Craig Mazin,
enlightens us (in under 140 characters):

---

\* Punishable by up to two years in prison, presumably without access to obscene
devices.

† "Oh, yeah?" we want to retort. "Then just whose genitals *can* one stimulate for such
purposes?"

Ted Cruz thinks people don't have a right to "stimulate their genitals." I was his college roommate. This would be a new belief of his.

Sorry. Please don't sue us for hurting your brain with the image of cheesy, unwholesome Ted Cruz whacking it in his dorm room, perhaps while fantasizing about a female member of an opposing Ivy League debate squad and...sorry!

Mazin, like pretty much everyone who has ever spent time with Cruz, can't stand him. Former House Speaker John Boehner called him "Lucifer in the flesh." "If you killed Ted Cruz on the floor of the Senate," said GOP senator Lindsay Graham, "and the trial was in the Senate, nobody would convict you."

But being universally despised does not necessarily make Cruz a monster. What makes him a monster is everything he's done, said, and thought. To avoid the need for a Cruz-and-nothing-but-Cruz companion volume, here's an abbreviated greatest-hits reel from his presidential campaign:

- Regarding ISIS, he said, "We will carpet-bomb them into oblivion. I don't know if sand can glow in the dark, but we're going to find out!" This, according to military experts, would mean killing everyone in a geographical area, including babies, mommies, and pets. The glowing sand part appears to mean Cruz thinks we should use nuclear weapons for our Middle Eastern carpet-bombing, in which case he's truly out of his fucking mind.
- He claimed to regret not having served in the military because, like all chicken hawks, he respects it immensely.
- He criticized **Donald** "I will build a wall!" **Trump** for being soft on immigration.

- He opposed abortion even in cases of rape or incest.
- He said he wants to return to the gold standard, which, as any actual economist knows, would melt the global economy.
- He cited as one of his signal accomplishments as the state's solicitor general his defense of the right of Texas to display a monument to the Ten Commandments.
- He endlessly repeated the line that he wants to abolish the IRS in favor of a simple flat tax that will allow Americans to file their taxes "on a postcard."*
- He enlisted conspiracy theorist Frank Gaffney, Jr., to advise him during his presidential run.
- He argued for a constitutional amendment allowing states to avoid recognizing same-sex marriages.
- He insisted that the minimum wage hurts poor people.
- He thought it witty to ridicule Trump's tepid support of the right of transgender people to use the bathroom of their choice with the line "Even if Donald Trump dresses up as Hillary Clinton, he still can't go to the girls' bathroom."

Despite the universally agreed upon signals that Cruz is intelligent—Princeton! Harvard!—there is a simple way to tell that he is not nearly as smart as he, or anyone else, thinks he is. As William Gaddis observed in his novel *Carpenter's Gothic*: "It's the smugness that's stupidity's telltale." Cruz's smugness is plastered across his face. It's always there, at least when he's in front of an audience. (His wife can tell us whether he's got that hideous "I know everything" expression on his face when he...

---

* As Cruz surely knows, the flat tax he (and a string of crackpots before him, such as STEVE FORBES) touts is a) wonderful for the top one percenters, not so much for the rest of us, and b) likely to reduce the government's revenues by as much as *$1 trillion a year* (which is probably why he likes it so much).

sorry! IGNORE! IGNORE!) What's so bad about being smug? Aside from making you look like Ted Cruz, it's an indicator that you are not interested in taking in any new information;* that you feel you know everything you need to know and have seen everything you need to see; that you have all the answers.

Which is pretty much the mandatory stance of a religious fundamentalist.

And that's fine if you're, say, a Dunkin' Donuts manager feeling smugly superior to the nine hell-bound flunkies you boss around. But if you're the kind of person who is absolutely certain that your truth is the only truth, then—sorry, Felito†— you're not the kind of person who should be in a position of actual power. At least not in the United States of America.

Dear reader, do tell us if you know of a fundamentalist dictatorship that Ted Cruz would like and—this is the hard part— where the citizens would like him. We'll be happy to crowdsource the funding to buy him a one-way ticket.

---

* Liberals tend to have a larger anterior cingulate gyrus—an area of the brain responsible for absorbing new information and integrating it with decision making—than do conservatives. Conservatives tend to have a larger right amygdala, a brain structure that is all about fear. Oh, you knew that? It's still worth mentioning.

† His childhood nickname, which he threw overboard when he tired of being teased about it. We think it's rather nice. "You been stimulating yourself, Felito?"

# Charles Davenport

*BA, Harvard University* ★ *PhD, Harvard University*

Dr. Charles Davenport defined eugenics as "the science of the improvement of the human race by better breeding." Who would dare argue with a double-degree Harvard man spouting such an immaculate tautology?

He was a bright lad whose youth was split between Brooklyn, New York, and rural Stamford, Connecticut. An interest in the natural world led him in his teens to assume the vice presidency of the Brooklyn chapter of the Agassiz Association, named for the famous Harvard biologist and bigot **Louis Agassiz**. In 1886, when Davenport was twenty, he graduated from Brooklyn Polytech with an engineering degree. Several months later the call of biology led him to enter Harvard — as a third-year undergrad — where, in relatively quick succession, he knocked off his BA and PhD. He then taught various biology classes at Harvard for six years, jumped to a better position at the University of Chicago, and, in 1904, talked the Carnegie Institution and Mary Harriman, of the railroad fortune, into funding his dream: the Station for Experimental Evolution* at Cold Spring Harbor, on Long Island, with him as director.

Davenport did some half-assed experiments with small lab animals and the like, but his obsession — driven by the rediscovery

---

\* You're reading that correctly.

of Gregor Mendel's theory of inheritance — was human evolution. There's no legal way to conduct human evolution experiments, of course. The "work-around" is to speculate endlessly, i.e., to make shit up. Which is exactly what Davenport did, accompanied by a superhuman cascade of paperwork in the form of pseudoscientific articles, papers, monographs, and books.

The overarching theme of his work was the protection of "American germ plasm" by encouraging "worthy" individuals to reproduce* while discouraging the "unworthy" of doing same. "Discouraging" meant two things: keeping unworthies out of the country, and sterilizing those who were already US citizens. (For more on sterilization, see **Harry Laughlin**, whom Davenport brought in to run his Eugenics Records Office.) Any guesses as to where Dr. Davenport's worthies came from† and what their skin looked like?

As early as 1911, the year before the First International Eugenics Congress,‡ a number of other biologists were debunking this bullshit for its bad science (for instance, its failure to understand that many traits have complex biological causes, and that some traits have no heritable causes or are the result of a complex nature-nurture interplay) and not-so-cleverly-concealed racism. That didn't slow down the eugenics juggernaut, which was taking on an increasingly religious flavor. At a certain point Davenport realized his Mosaic fantasy and attained his Mount Sinai moment by delivering his five-point Eugenics Creed unto the world. Here it is. We swear we're not making this up:

---

* More on this in a moment.

† Cough!…cough!…northernandwesterneurope!…cough!…cough!…

‡ Held in London and presided over, we're sorry to have to inform you, by Charles Darwin's son Leonard. That's *Major* Leonard Darwin to you.

- *I believe in striving to raise the human race to the highest plane of social organization, of cooperative work and of effective endeavor.*
- *I believe that I am the trustee of the germ plasm that I carry; that this has been passed on to me through thousands of generations before me; and that I betray the trust if (that germ plasm being good\*) I so act as to jeopardize it, with its excellent possibilities, or, from motives of personal convenience, to unduly limit offspring.†*
- *I believe that, having made our choice in marriage carefully, we, the married pair, should seek to have 4 to 6 children‡ in order that our carefully selected germ plasm shall be reproduced in adequate degree and that this preferred stock shall not be swamped§ by that less carefully selected.*
- *I believe in such a selection of immigrants as shall not tend to adulterate our national germ plasm with socially unfit traits.¶*
- *I believe in repressing my instincts\*\* when to follow them would injure the next generation.*

In 1918 Davenport and **Madison Grant** founded the Galton Society, a racist alternative to the American Anthropological Association. And in 1925 Davenport launched the International Federation of Eugenics Organizations, which included in its purview the Commission on Bastardization and Miscegenation.†† A few years later he introduced a global map

---

\* Know what I mean, wink wink, say no more, nudge nudge, know what I mean?

† Holy fuck.

‡ I.e., get busy, people. Assuming you are from northern or western Europe.

§ Holy fuck.

¶ Ibid. Because seriously. Nothing good can come from the phrase "to adulterate our national germ plasm."

\*\* Op. cit.

†† Sorry, we're fresh out of footnotes. Although we'd love to have heard how the receptionist answered the phone in that office.

of "mixed race" regions at an IFEO meeting held in Munich. Speaking of which...

You can bet that Austrian-born up-and-comer Adolf Hitler admired Davenport's work. And Davenport not only admired and supported Hitler and the fine work the Nazis did when they came to power, this upstanding American scientist became an editor of two German, which is to say Nazi, pseudoscience journals. Hitler freely credited American (largely Ivy League-educated) eugenicists with inspiring his Final Solution.

Eugenics started losing its luster in the United States as stories of Nazi atrocities crossed the Atlantic. It's nice to think that at some point Charles Davenport must have realized that future generations would forever link him with the silly-looking dictator widely considered to be the worst person who ever lived.

Davenport died of pneumonia in 1944, no doubt due to his inferior genes.

# Ira Einhorn

*BA, University of Pennsylvania*

*Einhorn,* as everyone knows, is German for "one horn." No wonder, then, that Ira Einhorn—the self-proclaimed house hippie for the city of Philadelphia in the 1960s and '70s— adopted the nickname "The Unicorn." In addition to Unicorn, Einhorn called himself a guru, a "catalyst for change," and—our favorite—"a planetary enzyme." He was stout (if not actually fat), bearded, and rarely bathed. (And yet women loved him—can somebody get back to us about that?) He was friends with, or at least an acquaintance of, Allen Ginsberg and Jack Kerouac; he hung out with Abbie Hoffman and Jerry Rubin.

He was also smart—he'd been a brilliant English major at Penn—nervy, and possessed the instincts of a con man or sociopath for self-promotion and telling people what they wanted to hear. He even consulted for businesses that wanted to know what the future would bring and how the counterculture could be exploited in the process. He spoke—after hijacking the stage for a half hour—at the first Earth Day rally in 1970. (He would later go on to say, falsely, that he "invented" Earth Day, a claim credulous and/or stupid right-wing sites still haul out to this very day.) He even, in 1977, held a fellowship at the Kennedy School of Government at (where else?) Harvard.

He met Holly Maddux, an ethereal beauty from Texas who had been a student at Bryn Mawr, in 1972. They moved in together. But in 1977, after five long years, sick of Ira's physical and verbal abuse, Maddux found refuge with a new boyfriend in New York. When she phoned Einhorn to so inform him, he insisted that she come back for her belongings immediately or he would dispose of them. She left for Philadelphia on September 9, 1977, and was never seen alive again.

Einhorn, of course, said he didn't know where she was. Her family didn't buy it. They hired private eyes. After two years, they came up with enough witness testimony to convince a judge to issue a search warrant. And lo: in a closet in Einhorn's apartment there was a trunk packed with newspapers, Styrofoam, "air fresheners," and the remains of Holly Maddux, partly mummified and now weighing thirty-seven pounds.

The Unicorn was arrested. And, really, only then does the story begin.

He was defended by none other than fellow Penn alum, former Philadelphia DA, and future Pennsylvania senator Arlen Specter, who wrangled enough influence and Philly oomph to get bail set at a paltry $40,000, of which Einhorn — or someone — had to pay only $4K. That someone was a woman named Barbara Bronfman, a Montreal socialite who had married into the uberwealthy family that owns Seagram's et al. Einhorn spent the ensuing months claiming that he was being framed by either the CIA or the FBI in order to discredit him and stop him from bringing down The Man. His narcissism was sufficiently vast that he may actually have believed that these government agencies thought he was some kind of James Bond villain.

Then, in January 1981, on the eve his pretrial hearing, Einhorn split the whole nowhere scene of his murder trial and disappeared. To where? That was the question. Charged with answering it was Assistant District Attorney Richard DiBennedetto, who had read sixty of Einhorn's journals and knew his man. In 1985 he traced Einhorn to Ireland, where the fugitive was living under the name of Ben Moore. By the time extradition papers could be drawn up, the Unicorn was gone again.

In 1993, in an unprecedented act—at least in Philadelphia—Einhorn was tried in absentia. He was found guilty of murder and sentenced to life. A year later, Barbara Bronfman confessed to DiBennedetto that she had not only been financing Einhorn's flight but that she knew where he'd fled: Stockholm. When the authorities arrived, they met a woman with the somewhat Jerry Lewis-ish name of Annika Flodin. She said she'd never heard of this Einhorn; she was living with a chap named Ben Moore. Then—don't ask—she slipped away. Finally, in June 1997, Ira and Annika were located in a village near Cognac, France, and the Unicorn was arrested.

End of Act II!

Act III opened with a whole lot of international legal wrangling (we assume with some woman somewhere paying Einhorn's legal bills) regarding extradition, the legality of a trial in absentia, human rights, and who knows what else. Finally, France and the USA agreed not to go to war over the Unicorn, and an extradition agreement was hammered out. Einhorn, realizing the jig was up, went all dramatic and slit his throat in front of TV cameras. Since the weapon in his hand was a butter knife, he survived the scratch and was soon on his way back to Philadelphia for a second trial.

During this proceeding, Einhorn informed the jurors that he "had a Virgo moon." Astonishingly, even that didn't help. In October 2002, six men and six women good and true found the Unicorn guilty of the murder of Holly Maddux. He was sentenced to life in prison without parole. District Attorney Lynn Abraham said, "Metaphorically speaking, Ira Einhorn and his Virgo moon are toast."

Einhorn is currently a long-term resident of Pennsylvania's Houtzdale State Correctional Institute.

# John Fairbanks

*BA, Dartmouth College*

Perhaps, after growing up a high-achieving child of a respected family in a respectable small town in New England, serving in the army in World War II, graduating from an Ivy League college, becoming an attorney (Boston University Law) and a part-time district court judge, and living what appeared to be an exemplary, small-town New England life with a wife and four children, John Fairbanks was finally rebelling. Or maybe he was just a bad human being with a stunted imagination, so it took him a long time to figure out how to let his bad-flag fly, and then the only transgressive thing he could think of was to steal money from people who trusted him.

Fairbanks graduated from Dartmouth in 1946, got his law degree in 1950, commenced the practice of probate and estate-planning law, and became a player in the New Hampshire Republican Party. *Snore…* But sometime during his decades of legal work, he *made* his life exciting. How? By stealing from his clients or their estates!

He was no Robin Hood. One victim was a blind retired farmer; another was an old woman on her deathbed. And there were insurance companies, a small bank, the town of Washington, New Hampshire, and three of *his own sisters*. In all, he stole as much as $10 million.*

---

\* There were also allegations that as a judge he traded sexual favors from male defendants in exchange for lighter sentences.

Local Democrats said there was plenty of evidence of his shenanigans* but claimed they couldn't act because the GOP old-boy network was shielding him. In 1989, however, the floodgates burst as more than twenty-five of his former clients (including his sisters!) filed more than $6 million worth of claims against him. Fairbanks resigned from the bench in June of that year. In August the New Hampshire Supreme Court suspended him from practicing law. Then, on December 27, he was indicted for his crimes.

The following day police arrived at his family's vacation place in Ogunquit, Maine, where Fairbanks had been holed up. But he had vanished. His wife said she had last seen him that morning when he'd gone downstairs for coffee. His story soon became a staple on TV crime shows like *America's Most Wanted*, and, predictably, people started phoning in tips, but none panned out. The man was off the radar and living on cash. Quite a bit of cash.

And then, on March 26, 1994, he turned up dead in a Las Vegas hotel room with a plastic bag over his head and a suicide note taped to the mirror.

The money never turned up: he presumably spent it all, then cashed himself in.

---

* We know — not nearly a strong enough word. How about wrongdoing? Criminality? Lawbreaking? Dickishness?

# Douglas Feith

*BA, Harvard University*

We start with a raging controversy: Did General Tommy Franks, commander of US Central Command and top military guy in the Middle East before, during, and after the invasion of Iraq, describe Douglas Feith as "the dumbest fucking guy on the planet," or as "the fucking stupidest guy on the face of the Earth"? It depends on your source. The first comes from Franks's autobiography, the latter from Bob Woodward's excitingly titled *Plan of Attack.*

Whatevs. The key thing is that you can graduate magna cum laude from Harvard, which Feith did, be spoken of by your peers as brilliant, and still find yourself tits-deep in (and supremely culpable for) the biggest, bloodiest, most costly fuckup since Vietnam. Or possibly since *ever.* And years later still be trying to worm your way out of responsibility.

Douglas Feith got his neocon feet wet and laid the groundwork for his eventual involvement in the Abu Ghraib fiasco when, as a Pentagon official in the 1980s, he propounded an argument that terrorists didn't deserve protection under the protocols of the Geneva Conventions. President Ronald Reagan agreed (so did the *New York Times* and the *Washington Post,* for that matter). Defense secretary Caspar Weinberger gave Feith a medal, and that was that, until **George W. Bush** was selected [*sic*] president. Bush, Vice President DICK "Darth" CHENEY, and the rest of Bush's foreign policy team met literally the day after Bush was inaugurated—i.e., eight months before 9/11—and discussed invading Iraq. Soon Feith was named undersecretary of defense for policy and, along with **Richard Perle** and PAUL WOLFOWITZ, began constructing the case for regime change in Iraq.

Feith worked with others to kick out Pentagon professionals who weren't as keen on whacking Saddam as they should have been, regardless of their experience and...you know...*knowledge*. Then 9/11 happened. It was one of the worst days in history for America, but it was the best thing that ever happened to George W. Bush (for a while, at least) and the neocon crowd. This was the excuse — or, rather, the foundation on which to construct a fake excuse — they had been waiting for.

An unnamed, secret unit was established in Feith's office to find or concoct disinformation to promote the war. While the CIA and the State Department concentrated on Osama bin Laden and al-Qaeda, Feith et al. obsessed about Saddam. Their thesis was roundly mocked and derided by people who had studied Saddam and counterterrorism for decades. There was no relationship between al-Qaeda and Iraq; Feith's and Paul Wolfowitz's labors to establish a connection led to the term "Feith-based intelligence."

But Feith and his buds persisted, creating two ad hoc desks in the Pentagon. The Counter Terrorism Evaluation Group's purpose was to "prove," via bogus intel and the revelations of paid liars, that Saddam was connected to 9/11. The Office of Special Plans would, after the invasion, be in charge of horribly bungling the occupation. It all worked in the sense that Wile E. Coyote's rampage off a cliff works: until he looks down.

When Feith was forced to look down, he did his best to persuade others (if not himself) that he wasn't plummeting to the ground. "When history looks back," he told Jeffrey Goldberg of *The New Yorker* in 2005, "I want to be in the class of people who did the right thing, the sensible thing, and not necessarily the fashionable thing, the thing that met the aesthetic of the moment." To Feith, then, opposing an unnecessary war was a matter of fashion and aesthetics. Uh-huh. Meanwhile, when Goldberg suggested that the deaths of "more than fifteen hundred soldiers"* was "a terrible loss," Feith took the larger view. Granting the horror of the loss to the families involved, he nonetheless persisted: "But this was an operation to prevent the next, as it were, 9/11, the next major attack that could kill tens of thousands or hundreds of thousands of Americans, and Iraq is a country of twenty-five million people and it was a major enterprise."

Feith said this two years after the rationale for the invasion — those pesky WMDs — had failed to materialize, and knowing that the "evidence" he had used to persuade the country to go to war had been hyped, faked, and long discredited.

Let's end with two quotes. When Goldberg pressed Feith on whether the administration was still unrealistically committed to the image of Iraqis welcoming the Americans with flowers, Feith said that some of the Iraqis were still too intimidated by Baath Party members to openly express themselves, but "they had flowers in their minds."

Then, gesturing to the books on Feith's shelves — "books," Goldberg writes, "by the great British Arabists, men such as T. E. Lawrence, John Bagot Glubb, and Harry St. John Philby" — the writer asks Feith what he's learned from them. Because don't neocons have "a certain nostalgia for the era of British

---

* Again, this was in 2005. The Watson Institute for International Studies at Brown University released a study calculating that the war cost US taxpayers $2.2 trillion and killed 4,488 members of the US armed services and at least 123,000 to 134,000 Iraqi civilians — this apart from the wounded, injured, traumatized, orphaned, and suicidal casualties on both sides.

imperialism"? Feith concedes that it helps to be deeply knowledgeable, but adds that that is no guarantee of having the right
strategy. "The great experts in certain areas sometimes get it
fundamentally wrong."

And then comes the punch line. "George W. Bush has more
insight, because of his knowledge of human beings and his
sense of history, about the motive force, the craving for freedom and participation in self-rule, than do many of the language experts and history experts and culture experts."

So there you have it. In the midst of the fiasco that was Iraq,
Douglas Feith praises the insight and the "knowledge of human
beings" of George W. Bush, the least curious, least insightful,
and least self-aware man in Washington.

What a dumb fucking guy.

# Thomas Gilbert, Jr.

*BA, Princeton University*

Tommy Gilbert was well born and well built. He not only looked like a particularly handsome surfer boy, he was an actual surfer—in the Hamptons! So perhaps it was  a combination of his looks, his parents' money, and his social connections that kept many of the people who knew him from reacting when he started losing his shit.

"I'm a graduate of Buckley," he wrote, in late 2015, in a letter to Manhattan DA Cyrus Vance, Jr. Buckley, which Gilbert and Vance† had both attended,‡ is a prep school on the Upper East Side; Gilbert also name-checked two more high-tuition alma maters, Deerfield Academy and Princeton. He sent the letter from the Manhattan Detention Complex—a.k.a. the Tombs—many blocks south of the Upper East Side. "Fortunately," he went on, "I've had access to the newspapers and have enjoyed reading articles about the DA's offices and the city's various cases. I was impressed by the overall decline in crime this summer." After the ass-licking, he gets down to business, complaining that he's not the sort of person who flourishes in jail, that he'd been

---

* We wanted to use *M* for *Murderer*, but our lawyer suggested *CP* for *Classification Pending*, because "Gilbert has not yet been tried and formally convicted of murder."

† Who went to Groton and Yale after his stint at Buckley, in case you're interested.

‡ A novel twist on old-boy networking.

"railroaded," and that he ought to be released to protect and preserve his "personal life" and his "career."

His career consisted mainly of sponging off his parents—he was thirty-one—while pretending to acquaintances that he was starting a hedge fund. As for his personal life, there were three outstanding episodes for which he was known.

- In October 2013 Gilbert had, for no reason, beaten the living shit out of Peter Smith, his Brooklyn roommate and fellow Buckley alum.
- Prior acts of violence and other circumstantial evidence led police to question Gilbert about the fire that, in September 2014, destroyed Peter Smith's family's lovely historic house in the Hamptons. As of this writing, Gilbert has not been charged and the case remains unresolved.
- On January 4, 2015, visiting his parents' Upper East Side apartment, he asked his mother to run out and fetch him a sandwich. That she complied and didn't say, "Either make one yourself or go out and fetch your own fucking sandwich" is, in and of itself, enough to make one think, "Jesus. These people." Then it got worse. Tommy Gilbert shot his father* point-blank in the head, placed the pistol on his dad's chest to make it look like a suicide, and left in a hurry.

He was arrested a short time later—hence his stay in the Tombs—in his own apartment in Chelsea.

He was said to be furious with his father for threatening to cut his $600 monthly allowance down to $400.†

---

* A Princeton grad with a Harvard MBA. He had worked on Wall Street for decades. For real. Pa Gilbert, at least, wasn't just making it up.

† Apparently Gilbert Senior intended to continue paying Junior's $2,400 monthly rent. Now Junior pays no rent! And gets his meals for free!

# Stephen Glass

*BA, University of Pennsylvania*

There are three ways for a journalist to write a story. In the first way, you go to where the story took place; you find out what happened and what didn't happen; you talk to the people involved; you do research into the background of the whole thing; and then you write it up, accurately, in your own words. In the second way, you *maybe* go to where the story took place. You maybe find out what did and didn't happen, and you maybe dig up some background. But you mainly avail yourself of the work of someone else who did it the first way. You copy and paste their work under your byline.

The first way has been traditionally referred to as "good old-fashioned shoe-leather reporting." The second way has been, and is, called "plagiarism."

In the third way, you just fucking make shit up. You invent stuff that didn't really happen. You interview fictional people via the wonders of the human imagination. Maybe you create background material, too—websites, story notes, other pseudodocumentation. Then you write it up—certainly in your own words, since no one else has ever heard of or reported on what you cobbled together in your head—and run it as fact.

This third way is called…well, various things. "Fraud." "Lies." "Willful deception." "A betrayal of your publication, your colleagues, and the public." And so on.

It is this third form of journalism that made Ivy League graduate Stephen Glass a household name—at least in households where people care about journalism—in 1998. Up until then, young Glass had had an excellent career as an editorial assistant, and then an Associate Editor, at *The New Republic*. In fact, Glass landed at *TNR* a mere year after being editor in chief of Penn's undergrad newspaper, the *Daily Pennsylvanian*.

Not only that, he began—at age twenty-three!—to contribute to *Policy Review*, *Harper's*, *Rolling Stone*, and *George*. Jonathan Chait and Hanna Rosin, his fellow *TNR* interns, marveled at Glass's talent, energy, and good luck in finding stories. Rosin writes, "While the rest of us were still scratching our way out of the intern pit, he was becoming a franchise, turning out bizarre and amazing stories week after week." Not everyone was thrilled. Organizations about which Glass had written (e.g., the Center for Science in the Public Interest, the College Republican National Committee, Drug Abuse Resistance Education, or D.A.R.E.) took sharp issue with what they called Glass's distortions and inaccuracies. Glass's editors defended him vigorously.

Then, in 1998, Associate Editor Glass published a story titled "Hack Heaven," about (scare-quote alert) "Ian Restil," a fifteen-year-old computer whiz who hacked his way into the networks of a company called Jukt Micronics. A writer for *Forbes*, pissed that his magazine had been scooped, looked into it—and discovered that "Jukt Micronics," when input into search engines, yielded not the usual 1,258,000 hits, but a big fat 0 hits. Jukt had exactly one phone line and a single tacky AOL webpage. By then, Glass's editor, the beloved Michael Kelly, had been replaced by the less colorful, more "grown-up" Charles Lane. Lane dragged Glass to the Hyatt Hotel in Bethesda, Maryland, where supposedly Restil had met with the Jukt guys. Lane asked questions and sought confirmations. But none of it panned out.

Stephen Glass had made the whole thing up. Impressively, he'd worked overtime to sell the fraud, from concocting the fake Jukt website to printing up bogus business cards. But when Lane realized that the "Jukt executive" he had spoken with on the phone was Glass's brother at Stanford, Lane fired Glass and ordered a review of all forty-one of the young man's pieces. At least twenty-seven of them turned out to have been partially, if not totally, fabricated. And while it wasn't the first or the last scandal of its kind in American journalism, it was arguably the most notorious one of the modern age.*

Bear in mind who is damaged by such behavior — because it turns out to be pretty much everybody. We, the readers, are, of course, deceived and misled. Any actual people who are written about falsely are slandered or traduced. The reputation of the publication involved is marred. And, just as bad, the fraudster's colleagues — who have probably trusted and defended him (or her) previously — are not only personally betrayed, but are left working for an institution with damaged credibility. Their work is suddenly cast in a bad light because some other guy broke the rules. Above and beyond that, this kind of behavior undermines journalism itself, providing ammunition to those who insist that it's *all* a pack of lies, when really, the lion's share of fiction-as-journalism is confined to the media vehicles owned by Rupert Murdoch.

After Stephen Glass was chased out of journalism, he went to law school and passed the bar in both New York and California, but neither state's bar association approved his application to practice. Today Glass works as a paralegal in the office of a Beverly Hills personal injury lawyer. He seems entirely repen-

---

* Although you could make a pretty good case for **Jonah Lehrer**.

tant, and we're open and forgiving enough to assume that that's sincere.

Still, one hopes that the next time he attends Penn, the school provides a mandatory class in "Not Violating Professional Ethics in a Way You *Have to Know* Will Inevitably Be Discovered."

# Al Gore

*BA, Harvard University*

W

Do we hold former vice president and presidential candidate Al Gore *entirely* responsible for the invasion of Iraq in 2003, the hundreds of thousands of Iraqi deaths, the nearly 4,500 casualties among American combatants, the tens of thousands of injured and damaged American troops, the more than *$2 trillion* the war has cost, and the myriad other fuckups associated with that misbegotten, irresponsible, reckless, stupid (and illegal) adventure? Not entirely. But *some*.

You may think us insane for even suggesting as much, but bear with us.

This worst-ever American foreign-policy decision was in fact led by Yale double-dropout* DICK CHENEY and his merry band of Iraq-crazed neocon chicken hawks, who populated the administration of President **George W. Bush**. Had Gore been president, it is inconceivable that he would have invaded Iraq on the basis of faked evidence that Saddam Hussein was behind the attacks of September 11, 2001. But — and it's a big but — if not for Al Gore, George W. Bush would not have been elected† president.

Bush "won" in Florida, and hence "won" the election, by a mere 537 votes. (We'll have more to say about this in our dis-

---

* Actually, he failed out twice, but "Yale double-failout" is not English. Although it does sound like a trick football play.

† Or however you choose to describe the process.

cussion of **Ralph Nader**.) As a presidential candidate, Gore was not a good campaigner. He was stiff and humorless, and for some reason he kept repeating the word "lockbox" whenever the cameras were rolling. "Lockbox! Lockbox!" (We think it had something to do with Social Security.) But Gore had a formidable weapon at his disposal. He'd been the vice president of **Bill Clinton,** one of the greatest campaigners ever, who was ready, willing, and able to hit the hustings for his VP. Did Gore deploy this weapon? No, he did not. In fact, he avoided Clinton the way a lottery winner avoids a grifter cousin. Why? Because Bill had been impeached by the GOP morality squad. Clinton and his high approval rating survived, but Gore didn't want to have his own prissy little image sullied by the president's peccadillos.

Would a campaign-long boost from Clinton have lifted Gore enough in Florida to overcome that 537-vote deficit? Hmm. In a quick wormhole-hop over to a certain parallel universe we know, we observed that, yes, Gore, with Clinton's help, beat Bush by a comfortable margin in Parallel Florida. So that's settled.

But wait! There's more! In addition to having Bush's brother Jeb on hand as governor and chief enforcer of Florida, the GOP sent its A-team of unscrupulous bullyboys and dirty tricksters to oversee the recount. When Gore finally conceded, it wasn't because everyone was satisfied that the recount was fair and Bush had legitimately won. It was because of a supine media, a supine Florida legislature, and the Supine—sorry; the *Supreme* Court* of the United States, which stopped the recount, ratified the work of the bullyboys, and handed the election to Bush. That's when Gore dropped the option of pushing on with the

---

* On which sat two justices appointed by the father of the winning candidate.

recount, gave up, and curtseyed graciously to fellow Ivy League alum W—despite having won both the national and the Florida popular vote.*

One more thing. Who(m) had Gore picked as his running mate? Why, **Joe Lieberman,** who had been the very first Democratic senator to parachute in from the moral high ground to join the Republican impeachment squad† in wagging their fingers at Bill Clinton. Why choose someone so obnoxious and so whiny that having him on the ticket must have driven down Gore's numbers by a nontrivial percentage? Because Gore wanted Lieberman's self-righteous ass right there next to him, as proof of his own moral worthiness. Which must also be the reason for that cringy, practically openmouthed kiss Gore and his (now estranged) wife, Tipper,‡ shared at the Democratic convention. We're in love! There'll be no out-of-wedlock splooging in the White House when I'm president! Lockbox! Lockbox!

And then came 9/11 and the shit-show of the George W. Bush years. No, Al Gore wasn't responsible for all of that. But if he'd made a few better decisions—using more of his brain and spine, less of his good manners—none of it would have come to pass.

Personal message to Al Gore: Stay away from politics. Continue saving the Earth.

---

* Remember the "butterfly ballot" issue, in which thousands of Gore voters mistakenly voted for right-winger Pat Buchanan? We don't either.

† A squad that included Denny Hastert, sexual abuser of students; adulterer Henry Hyde; and multiadulterers Newt Gingrich and Bob Livingston.

‡ She of the sanctimonious campaign for nasty-language warning labels on records.

# Madison Grant

*BA, Yale University ★ LLB, Columbia University*

In 1924, imprisoned for leading the failed coup d'état known as the Beer Hall Putsch, corporal Adolf Hitler passed his time working on *Mein Kampf* and reading inspirational books by American eugenicists. Among his favorites was *The Passing of the Great Race,* written by Madison Grant eight years earlier. The corporal even wrote the author a fan letter. "The book," said Hitler, "is my Bible."*

Grant was a well-known eugenicist and conservationist,† but he was not a scientist. What credibility he had derived solely from his upper-class pedigree, his Ivy League education, and his inherited wealth.‡ Described by a contemporary as "the most lordly of patricians," Grant practiced law for a couple of years, but, realizing he had more important things to accomplish, and with no need for an income, he stopped working and devoted the rest of his life to his two hobbyhorses. And to schmoozing§ with like-minded aristocrats at

---

\* Which enshrined it as one of the all-time top-ten books for morons. The Norwegian psychopath who murdered sixty-nine kids in 2011 mentioned Grant's book in his own depraved manifesto. For zoologist Stephen Jay Gould, *Great Race* was "the most influential tract of American scientific racism."

† Odd combo, you think? Read on, O Noble Reader!

‡ Thank God *that* no longer obtains in our modern, sensible society.

§ This is not a word he would have used. What are you, meshuggah?

his exclusive Manhattan clubs, the Century, Tuxedo, University, Knickerbocker, and Union.

The "great race" in his book's title does not refer to a slapstick automobile competition from New York to Paris featuring an epic pie fight, alas. Rather, it refers to the "race"* of which Grant believed himself to be an upstanding member. If you're thinking this must be "white," well, sure, but it's more complicated — and exclusive — than that. Mr. Grant, you see, had carefully read *The Races of Europe* by **William Z. Ripley,** which preposterously posited that there were three European races: Teutonic, Mediterranean, and Alpine. Grant changed Teutonic to "Nordic," crowned it the race of "the white man *par excellence,*" and whined in the pages of his masterwork that the inferior types streaming into the United States from Mediterranean and Alpine locales were intermarrying with the good, pure Nordic people and diluting their grade-A blood. Not to mention the catastrophe that the Jew and Negro vermin were bringing down on the nation.

The solution? In harmony with others who shared his beliefs, Grant advocated keeping the bad ones out with a "Nordics Only" immigration policy and sterilizing many of the bad ones who had already slipped in. And was he ever strict! "Mistaken regard for what are believed to be divine laws and a sentimental belief in the sanctity of human life," he wrote, "tend to prevent both the elimination of defective infants† and the sterilization of such adults as are themselves of no value to the community." Grant also, quite logically, suggested the creation of special zones — call them "ghettos" or "concentration

---

* In quotation marks because there's no such thing, scientifically speaking.

† One can imagine Grant-inspired posters in hospitals reading "Don't Be Sentimental. Destroy Defective Infants."

camps"—for the confinement of loser genes and those who carry them.

It's difficult for us, a century later, to understand that Grant and the others who spouted off like this were, in their day, *progressives*, attempting to make the world a better place. Unfortunately, their concept of "the world" was cartoonishly narrow.* To them "the world" meant "the good people" or "people like us" or "the Nordics." Everyone else was—not to put too fine a point on it—an unfit mongrel subhuman.

Add to this what we'll call their genetic hubris—pride in their own chromosomal endowments coupled with the belief that they, the cream of humanity, the holders of prestigious degrees, the scientists, finally had more influence over evolution than natural selection itself—and the relationship between eugenics and conservation is clear: conservation was to the various species of the natural world what eugenics was to the human species. Both were about tailoring the landscape, in the broadest sense of the word, to the tastes of their class.

Which meant preserving certain animals (mainly big ones like bison and bear), plants (big trees like the California redwoods), and humans (Nords) while expressing no interest in the less "aristocratic" varieties (squirrels, pachysandra, Alpiners, Mediterraneans, the dark skinned...). In this, Grant was not so much an outlier as a blustery mouthpiece for the received wisdom of his tribe. As another tribe member, Theodore Roosevelt (Harvard BA), gushed in a letter to Grant that *The Passing of the Great Race* was "a capital book; in purpose, in vision, in grasp of the facts our people† most need to realize." The passage was

---

* See **Abbott Lawrence Lowell** for more in this cartoonishly narrow vein.

† IYKWHMAWTTYD (If You Know What He Meant And We Think That You Do).

excerpted and splashed on the cover of the book's next edition.

In fairness—and we're nothing if not fair—Madison Grant was instrumental in the founding of a number of important American institutions, including the American Museum of Natural History, the Bronx Zoo, the Save the Redwoods League, Glacier and Denali National Parks, and the American Bison Society. For these he deserves a soupçon of praise, especially since today these organizations back away from mentioning his name as if doing so would infect them with Zika.

His batshit racial prescriptions for the nation, on the other hand, fell short of expectations. Wouldn't it be fun to dig Grant up, breathe life into him for a few hours, drag his sorry zombie ass to the Museum of Natural History, and torture him by sticking him in a diorama for busloads of multihued schoolkids to gawk at?

# Dr. Dirk Greineder

*BA, Yale University* ★ *Assistant Professor, Harvard University*

He was born in Germany in 1940, which wasn't such a great time to be born in Germany. His parents managed to whisk him away to Lebanon, where he grew up speaking German, Arabic, French, and English. He was a bright young man—bright enough* to get into Yale, where he commenced his studies in 1958. He was a dedicated chemistry major who made time for athletics and, according to classmates, had an eye for the ladies. After Yale he went on to medical school at Case Western Reserve in Cleveland, was a workaholic, and eventually rose to the august post of director of clinical allergy at Harvard affiliate Brigham and Women's Hospital in Boston. He also taught at Harvard. He was married to a lovely woman, had three lovely kids, and lived in a lovely house in ritzy, lovely suburban Wellesley. In 1997 he won the lovely Harvard Pilgrim Health Care Outstanding Physician Award. Life was good—lovely, even—for Dr. Dirk Greineder.

There was one issue, if you can call it that. At some point a sexual Mr. Hyde emerged from the murky depths of the doctor's, uh, soul. This was a computer-savvy Mr. Hyde who, by cleverly manipulating the keyboard of Dr. Greineder's computer, downloaded heroic quantities of online pornography, arranged rendezvous with prostitutes, enrolled the doctor in a dating service, and introduced the doctor to online swingers,

---

* It probably didn't hurt that he spoke all those languages and was applying from exotic Lebanon.

including a couple looking to experiment with a venturesome third party. He also wrote Viagra prescriptions for the fifty-something Dr. Greineder.

Which is not to imply that Greineder actually had a multiple-personality disorder, or that "Mr. Hyde" was the name of the good doctor's fiendish alter ego. No, that happened to be "Thomas Young," a name borrowed from a Yale classmate Greineder hadn't seen in many years. The alter ego had his own credit cards, which paid for everything from hot-sheet hotel rooms to calls to 1-900 phone-sex lines.*

There are no doubt many ostensibly happily married men whose computers would reveal similar browsing histories and cookie trails. Are they all wife murderers? What are you, crazy? Which is the point his lawyer made at Greineder's murder trial: my client may have been a degenerate sex addict,† but that doesn't mean he killed his wife.

Yes, Mabel Greineder — May to friends — was murdered on Halloween morning 1999, near bucolic Morses Pond in Welles-ley. The story her husband told is that he and May had taken one of their dogs for a walk; May somehow wrenched her back, so she rested on a rock while he continued walking the dog; he returned in a little while to find her dead, in the woods, with multiple stab wounds, her skull smashed, her throat slashed. He claimed that he tried to revive her — he had been an emergency-room doc for years — but he was too late. It must have been a mystery assailant, he theorized.

At least two books have been written on the crime and the trial, and barrels of newspaper ink have been spilled detailing the evidence that convicted Greineder of murder. Readers who

---

* How far we've come from those ancient days!

† We paraphrase.

wish to follow up are free to dig *even deeper than we have dug*, if you can imagine such a thing.

Meanwhile, we'll stick with these telling bits:

- Police found a bloody hammer, a knife, and a pair of gloves near the crime scene. Greineder was covered in May's blood when the police arrived *but his hands were clean*. The prosecution alleged, sensibly, that he'd had the gloves on when he killed her, then took them off and — unsuccessfully — disposed of them. If he'd actually tried to revive her, the argument went, his hands would have been at least as bloody as the rest of him.
- There were no mystery-assailant footprints in the area, just Greineder's.
- DNA evidence linked Greineder to the hammer, knife, and gloves.

As we said, Greineder's sexual proclivities do not mean that he killed his wife. But the crime scene evidence does. That established, here are two more bullet points to contemplate.

- The weekend before the murder, Dr. Greineder spent time with a hooker in a hotel in New Jersey. He must have really liked her because…
- *The day after his wife's murder* he called to schedule another tryst with the same prostitute.

His position, current at the time of this writing, is Vice Chairman with an Emphasis on "Vice" of the Lifers' Group at the Massachusetts Correctional Institution in Norfolk.

# Edward Holyoke

*BA, Harvard University ★ MA, Harvard University*
*★ President, Harvard University*

Edward Holyoke was born into a wealthy family in colonial Massachusetts — wealthy enough, in fact, that Mount Holyoke, the *actual mountain*,* as well as the town of Holyoke, were named after his grandfather. Edward graduated from Harvard in 1705 at age sixteen, picked up his MA three years later, worked at Harvard for several years as a librarian and then an instructor, and in 1716 finally left Harvard to become pastor of a church in Marblehead. He stayed away from Harvard until 1730, when the governor of the Province of Massachusetts Bay lured him back by appointing him the ninth president of Harvard, in which post he stayed until his death in 1769.

Holyoke was a good college president. Among other improvements, he navigated the school away from the religious orthodoxy under which it had been founded, strengthened math and science teaching, introduced a physics lab, raised money, added to the infrastructure, and introduced merit-based admissions.

But here's the thing. While he was president of Harvard, Edward Holyoke owned two human beings of African extraction. They lived in the presidential residence, Wadsworth House, along with Holyoke and his family. Their names were Juba and Bilhah. They did not have last names.

---

* As opposed to Mount Holyoke College, which was named after the mountain that was named after his grandfather.

In 2007, Harvard students* of diverse ethnic backgrounds initiated an investigation into the school's relationship with slavery over its first couple of centuries. According to the Harvard and Slavery website,

> Much of what they found was surprising: Harvard presidents who brought slaves to live with them on campus, significant endowments drawn from the exploitation of slave labor, Harvard's administration and most of its faculty favoring the suppression of public debates on slavery.

Nothing can be done to change that history, of course, but dredging it to the surface and finding ways to criticize and memorialize it may help current and future Harvard dwellers feel better about themselves. One tangible result of the investigation is the large plaque on display at Wadsworth House that Harvard president Drew Gilpin Faust† unveiled in April 2016. It pays tribute to what Faust called the "stolen lives" of Juba and Bilhah, as well as those of Titus and Venus, who were slaves of Holyoke's predecessor and presidential-house eponym **Benjamin Wadsworth.**

Among many others, the distinguished Harvard professor Henry Louis Gates, Jr.,‡ was there to bear witness to the event.

---

* All of whom had last names.

† Who is a woman and not a man.

‡ Some of whose ancestors were African. They did not leave Africa of their own volition.

# Stephen Hopkins

*Brown University Benefactor*

Stephen Hopkins was a boldface name — arguably Rhode Island's number-one notable — in the decades leading up to the American Revolution. Born into a well-established Providence family* in 1707, his father and grandfather presented him with 160 acres of farmland in nearby Scituate, Massachusetts, when he was nineteen; by age twenty-three the ambitious young man was not only a farmer but a local justice of the peace. Looking to live a little larger, he sold the farm in 1742 and moved back to town, where he entered the mainstream of Providence life as a shipbuilder, ship outfitter, ship owner, and import-export merchant. Later on he went into the iron foundry business in partnership with the **Brown Family**. Within five years of his move to Providence he was a justice of the Rhode Island Supreme Court; then chief justice; and in 1755 he became the governor of what was then called the Colony of Rhode Island and Providence Plantations.

Always a studious sort, Hopkins was a stout supporter,† and the first chancellor, of the College of Rhode Island (later known as Brown University) from its founding in 1764. In 1765, the

---

* His great-grandfather was one of the original settlers of Providence in the 1630s. You can't get more established than that…unless, you know, your people had been living there for a thousand years before the Europeans came along.

† He was the most generous of the college's founding donors.

British Parliament passed the Stamp Act,* a nasty piece of work designed to control commerce and suck money, in the form of taxes and duties, out of the colonies. To counter this sort of financial oppression, Hopkins wrote a pamphlet entitled *The Rights of Colonies Examined,* published by the Rhode Island General Assembly. It was a rousing, widely distributed success, a foundational document in American-revolutionary thinking. A decade later, Hopkins was among those who signed the Declaration of Independence.

Thus far, we have portrayed him as an unalloyed hero of the revolution. But there's one important detail we left out.

*The Rights of Colonies Examined* includes these thoughts: "Liberty is the greatest blessing that men enjoy, and slavery the heaviest curse that human nature is capable of.... Those who are governed at the will of another, and whose property may be taken from them...without their consent...are in the miserable condition of slaves."

So Hopkins was well aware that slavery was a terrible thing. A curse. Which is ironic, to say the least, as Hopkins was involved in casting that very curse on other human beings. He owned at least five slaves.† And, like pretty much everyone‡ in Rhode Island in the 1700s, he profited, at least indirectly, from the slave trade: building ships, outfitting ships, owning ships... need we say more? And that iron foundry he co-owned with the

---

* A precursor of the infamous Tea Act of 1773, which spawned the Boston Tea Party, which led inexorably to the American Revolution, which has nothing whatsoever to do with the ignoramuses who, after the election of the first black president of the US in 2008, went all batshit and started calling themselves Tea Partiers.

† This was far from rare in ye olde Rhode Island. The REVEREND JAMES MANNING, the first president of the college later known as Brown, for instance, was accompanied by his own slave when he arrived.

‡ Except slaves, we need hardly point out.

Brown family: ship fittings, shackles, chains....Speaking of the Browns, Stephen Hopkins's brother, Esek,* was the captain of one of their slave ships. Not that we expect Stephen to have been Esek's keeper, but it does show that there was only the tiniest degree of separation between those who trafficked directly in slaves and those who merely kept some slaves of their own while profiting from the sale of shackle-and-chain ensembles.

As the revolution approached, Hopkins came to the realization that the curse of slavery was incompatible — duh!, yes, but not everyone reached the same conclusion, obviously — with the quest to build a new country founded on freedom and equality. In 1774, he introduced an early antislavery bill and started setting his own slaves free.

Better late than never, Mr. Hopkins.

---

* This is not a typo.

# E. Howard Hunt

*BA, Brown University*

> *He was a complete self-centered WASP who saw himself as this blue blood.... "I'm better than anybody because I'm white, Protestant and went to Brown, and since I'm in the CIA, I can do anything I want." Jew, nigger, Polack, wop—he used all those racial epithets. He was an elitist. He hated everybody.*
> — HOWARD HUNT'S SON SAINT JOHN HUNT,
> IN ROLLING STONE

The "E" is for "Everette," which is a disturbing name for a macho-man spy, especially with that girly "ette" ending. No wonder he abbreviated it. But the silly name isn't what's surprising about E. Howard Hunt. What's surprising—if you're familiar with Hunt as one of Richard Nixon's dirty tricksters—is that he was a novelist. A prolific one. He wrote at least forty books, mostly under his own name but also as Robert Dietrich, P. S. Donoghue, David St. John, and John Baxter. We don't know how good a living he could have made had he focused on his writing career. But if he had—unless his writing was exceptionally bad—he probably wouldn't have ended up spending thirty-three months in a federal prison camp.

Born in 1918 to ultra-WASPy parents in the middle of nowhere (Hamburg, New York), he majored in English at Brown. During the war he served in the navy, then as an intelligence officer for the OSS, precursor to the CIA. Joining the incipient CIA in 1949, he became station chief in Mexico City the following year; there he supervised another Ivy League grad and fellow rabid-anticommie **William F. Buckley.** Let's have a look at some highlights of his CIA and post-CIA career:

- He worked on the 1954 coup that overthrew the president of Guatemala, leading to forty years of repression and 200,000 Guatemalan deaths. When later asked how he felt about that grisly body count, Hunt responded: "Deaths? What deaths?"
- He was deeply involved in the Bay of Pigs invasion — traditionally referred to as "the abortive Bay of Pigs invasion" — of Cuba in 1961. The operation was an abysmal flop. Hunt was removed from field operations — i.e., spying — and given an office job as assistant to Allen Dulles, director of Central Intelligence (and a Princeton man), where he reportedly worked on Dulles's book *The Craft of Intelligence.*
- His exile to the director's office didn't last long. The CIA was meant to operate outside the boundaries of the United States, but after the Bay of Pigs failure the Kennedy administration launched the Domestic Operations Division, with Hunt as its chief of covert action. His primary mandate was to manipulate the news by feeding reporters false information or bribing them. Hunt later admitted that this homefront propaganda mission violated the CIA's charter. He left the agency for good in 1970.
- In 1971 he was hired by Nixon's special counsel (and future pious penitent) Chuck Colson (another Brown man) to put his CIA experience to work for Tricky Dick as a member of the president's covert Special Investigations Unit, better known as the White House Plumbers. So called because their task was to stop leaks. Yeah, "ha ha." Look, it's Republican humor. The leak that started it all was the set of classi-

fied documents, which came to be known as the Pentagon Papers, that Daniel Ellsberg (Harvard BA, PhD) slipped to the *New York Times* and eighteen other newspapers.* Why was Nixon irked that these documents were going public? Because they provided tons of evidence that the government can't be trusted!

- Hunt's first assignment as a Plumber: break into the office of Daniel Ellsberg's shrink and steal the shrink's notes on the patient. The idea was to discredit Ellsberg and, incidentally, punish him for what he'd done. The operation was not only a miserable failure — Hunt either never found the notes or Nixon's gang couldn't figure out what to do with them — it was the reason the espionage case against Ellsberg was dismissed: government misconduct.

- When Ellsberg's espionage charges were dismissed, Hunt concocted another plot to discredit him, this time by slipping him a dose of LSD before he spoke at an antiwar event.† The Cuban waiters he hired to slip the payload into Ellsberg's soup (true story) couldn't get to the event on time, and the mission was aborted.

- Finally, Hunt's crowning, and final, dirty trick: the Watergate break-in, in which he and evil genius G. Gordon Liddy organized a team‡ to enter the Democratic National Committee headquarters in the Watergate complex to photograph documents and bug phones. They were busted by a security guard, the FBI traced them to Hunt, a cover-up was uncovered, Woodward and Bernstein followed the money, and soon everyone watched Nixon on the nightly news as he

---

* Think of them as news-filled websites, but made of paper. Hence the term.

† "You antiwar people are so beautiful, and these colors, I can feel the universe breathing, wow, look at my hand, it's pulsing, it's part of the breathing universe…"

‡ Composed of exiled Cubans Hunt knew from his Bay of Pigs fuckup.

skulked across the White House lawn, awkwardly (and irrationally, absurdly) flashed the V sign, and climbed into the Marine chopper for the last time.

- Hunt went to prison for Watergate. Until the day he died, in 2007, he remained bitter that he was punished while Nixon remained a free — if disgraced — man. He never quite understood that being a white, Protestant Brown alum doesn't mean you own the country.

He was a high-spirited 30-year-old novelist who aspired to wealth and power when he joined the C.I.A. in 1949. He set out to live the life he had imagined for himself, a glamorous career as a spy. But Mr. Hunt was never much of a spy. He did not conduct classic espionage operations in order to gather information. His field was political warfare: dirty tricks, sabotage and propaganda.

— From Hunt's *New York Times* obituary

But he did leave a sort-of-literary legacy: thanks to his last big, bungled burglary, we began to append the word "-gate" to every political scandal, real or bogus. And we still do, to this very day.

# Laura Ingraham

*BA, Dartmouth College*

As the book of Ecclesiastes and Pete Seeger and the Byrds have told us, "To every Coke / Turn, turn, turn / There is a Pepsi / Turn, turn, turn / And a Burger King to ev'ry McDonald's / Under Heaven." (That's why capitalism is so great, in case you didn't know.) Thus, for every Ann Coulter, there is a Laura Ingraham. Which is to say — and meaning absolutely no disrespect to Pepsi or Burger King — that Laura Ingraham is a lesser Coulter: an Ivy-educated, blond conservative "commentator" (read: propagandist) who, although not quite as successful, famous, or appalling as Coulter, is certainly in her hideous league.

In college Ingraham wrote for the *Dartmouth Review,* the first of the really elegant, repellent conservative Ivy League journals. The *Review* became the template for similar publications at Harvard, Princeton, Yale, and Cornell, each providing a political home and journalistic platform by which eighteen-to-twenty-one-year-old pishers could, by aping their elders and betters,* audition for a wingnut-welfare sinecure.

In her senior year at Dartmouth Ingraham became the *Review*'s first female editor in chief. She was virulently homophobic. The maga-

---

\* See **William F. Buckley.**

zine's faculty advisor ascribed to her "the most extreme anti-homosexual views imaginable." One time, for instance, she dispatched an undercover reporter to attend a meeting of the Gay Students Association, then published a transcript of the meeting. Years later, in a *Washington Post* op-ed, she defended herself:

> Part of what we did was journalistically justifiable: The group received college funding but, unlike every other student group receiving a college grant, refused to make public its membership or budget. We wanted to find out how student funds were being spent and to demonstrate the double standard Dartmouth had created by funding the group. But in doing so, we adopted a purposefully outrageous tone — occasionally using, for example, the word "sodomites" to describe campus gays.

Got that? We were concerned about student funds, so we called people "sodomites," just as, had we been concerned about the use of student funds by Hillel House, we would have referred to its Jewish members as "Christ-killers." That purposefully outrageous tone, we find, accomplishes so much.

Ingraham minimizes this as being one of her *"Dartmouth Review* antics," as though similar to other college-age hijinks like be-ins, binge-drinking pukefests, or panty raids. Besides, the point of the piece was to talk about the change of heart she experienced during the previous ten years.

First, you see, her gay brother, Curtis, had come out to her. Over time, both he and his AIDS-afflicted partner displayed "dignity, fidelity and courage" as they coped with the disease. So moved was Ingraham that her "views and rhetoric" regarding homosexuality were "tempered."

Damn decent of her, innit? Then again: If you condemn a behavior because you think it immoral ("sodomite" isn't a political term; it's a moralizer's term), why should the *dignity* of its practitioners make any difference? Or do you relent only because the practitioner is your brother? And if gay men's dignity tempers your disapproval, then how valid and dependable was—and is—the source of your moral judgments in the first place?

Ingraham doesn't get that far in the article. Still, she does write, "I now regret that at Dartmouth we didn't consider how callous rhetoric can wound." Yes, it sounds like a note of apology your mother made you give a neighbor for smashing into his mailbox, but still: isn't that nice?

Well... That op-ed is twenty years old. We've had two decades to wonder, What has sadder, wiser, more tolerant Laura Ingraham been up to since? Has she used her change of mind regarding sexuality—to the extent that it's sincere, and not limited to members of her immediate family—as a lens through which to study her *other* reactionary opinions? If she was wrong about gays, is she perhaps wrong about other things, too?

As the French say, *fat chance*. Why jeopardize a cushy gig? Like other right-wing radio hosts who make a good buck spreading hate and stoking rage under the guise of defending conservative values, Ingraham makes her living trashing liberals, deploring America's cultural decline, feigning working-class solidarity by mocking Hollywood and that old demagogue's standby, "elites," and doing her bit to assure that the decent, God-fearing people on the right remain as indignant, outraged, and oblivious as ever.

Here, from 2016, is an Ingraham contribution to the transgender-restroom conversation:

We have a new transgender update...for all of you who are bathroom-goers and public—you use public restrooms? I think a lot of people are going to be walking around with just Depends on from now on. They're just not going to use the bathroom. Adult diapers, diapers for everybody....Then you'll be in your own bathroom. Everyone's bathroom is just their own clothes, OK?

And here's a nice piece of good, honest, old-time demagoguery she dispensed in March 2016, when she agreed with someone on a radio call-in program who endorsed Donald Trump's view of Mexicans.

Well, they have come here....Yeah, they have come here to murder and rape our people. We know that. That doesn't mean everybody has, doesn't mean everyone who comes across the border is a nasty, horrible person, but they have violated our laws.

It's one thing to be a provocateur. It's another to provoke resentment all the livelong day by broadcasting callous rhetoric—which, as someone once said, can wound. But it sure beats working—and, to the extent that Ingraham is rich and famous, she does Dartmouth proud.

# Arthur Jensen

*PhD, Columbia University*

For years, many of America's elite private schools used the Wechsler Preschool and Primary Scale of Intelligence (WPPSI-R) as an admissions hurdle for four-year-olds. (No, not fourteen. *Four.*) Perhaps some still do. The schools justified this IQ test by saying it was a good predictor of academic success and therefore a valuable guide to who should or shouldn't be invited in. Indeed, years of tracking showed the WPPSI-R to correlate fairly well with future academic success, from elementary school performance right up through college and beyond. Little kids who did well on the test tended to become successful, well-compensated adults.

However, as some experts in the field pointed out, there's a simpler, more effective way to judge whether a four-year-old will be a paragon of achievement: just look at the parents' tax returns. It turns out that parents' income is more highly correlated than the WPPSI-R—or any test—with a youngster's odds of succeeding in life. It's not about money per se. It's about what people with adequate resources can provide a child— materially, intellectually, maybe even spiritually—to set that child up for a successful life, and how those lacking the resources often cannot. Since the schools were not about to demand prospective parents' tax returns,* the test was a good, seemingly anodyne, scientific-style substitute.

---

* It wouldn't look good. "How much money you make? Okay, that's good enough, your kid's in. Next."

What is it that IQ tests test? The simple, if jejune,* answer is: IQ tests test your ability to take IQ tests. Since these tests are written by highly educated members of the dominant culture, with little thought to what members of less dominant subcultures might or might not know, a more substantive answer might be: IQ tests gauge how well various elements of the dominant culture are integrated into your consciousness. Books are written on this subject, but this isn't one of them. Instead, let us segue to Berkeley prof Arthur Jensen, PhD.

Focusing on educational psychology, Jensen made his bones by unambiguously coming down on the side of nature in the perennial nature vs. nurture debate. It's a profoundly conservative stance: if nature — genetics — conquers all, then belief in the whole hopey-changey thing (a.k.a. "progress") is pointless. You are the way you are because of your ancestors. Live with it. And shut up.

Perhaps that's a bit overstated. Jensen didn't say that nature conquers all. He said that nature conquers 80 percent of all. In a 1969 paper in the *Harvard Educational Review* that caused a considerable amount of drooling among fair-skinned reactionaries, he concluded that Head Start programs had failed in their quest to boost the average IQ of dark-skinned schoolchildren. This, he said, was because 80 percent of the variance in IQ scores was attributable to the genetic endowments of the test population. In other words, their genes are encoded for stupidity and they are therefore 80 percent condemned to be stupid, regardless of how much preschool "enrichment" they're exposed to.

Jensen's work was widely criticized; there were protests out-

---

* We've been waiting for a chance to use that word.

side his office at Berkeley.* But away from coddled-liberal enclaves, his material killed. The Pioneer Fund, founded by a rich crackpot† who was devoted to eugenics, and was once presided over by **Harry Laughlin,** contributed more than $1 million‡ to further Jensen's "research."

One way to tell whether you are an actual scientist rather than a scientific racist is to ask yourself: "Would I take grant money from an entity whose sole purpose is to promote racism, or would I eschew such an unsavory source, soldier on in my attempts to gain less tainted funding, and occasionally complain bitterly and publicly that my work is being misunderstood by racist assholes?" Whether or not Jensen asked that question of himself, what he said to the Pioneer Fund was: "Thank you for your kind contribution."§

And so, back to IQ testing. Jensen's premise — behind all the sciency noise about the sad, sad state of African Americans' IQs — was that IQ is a real thing that really means something, really. He even concocted a make-believe genetic component, which he laughably christened "the g¶ factor," and which he claimed had a lot to do with the difference between the IQs of blacks and whites. Think of it this way: the g factor is to IQ what IQ is to tax returns. To put it scientifically:

$$\frac{\text{the } g \text{ factor}}{\text{IQ}} = \frac{\text{IQ}}{\text{tax returns}}$$

---

* Which, at Berkeley, was not that big a deal.

† WICKLIFFE DRAPER.

‡ It also gave at least a couple of million to other researchers cited in **Charles Murray**'s *The Bell Curve,* which cites Jensen twenty-three times.

§ Dialogue simulated.

¶ That's an italicized lowercase *g,* which stands for — hold your breath — *"genetic"*! Or *"genetic component"*! Or something equally *gobsmacking.*

Which means that:

$$IQ^2 \quad = \quad \text{(the } g \text{ factor)(tax returns)}$$

So, solving for IQ:

$$IQ \quad = \quad \sqrt{\text{(the } g \text{ factor)(tax returns)}}$$

Finally, a clear definition of IQ! It is shocking and surprising that Arthur Jensen did not devise this brilliant, enigmatic formula himself, considering that those who did, the authors of the present volume, know next to nothing about the subject. On the other hand, if Jensen had promulgated such a formula we probably would never have heard of him, he would not have caused near riots at Berkeley, and he would not have become a grant magnet and icon of the racist right.

# Piyush "Bobby" Jindal

*BS, Brown University*

After MITT ROMNEY's defeat in 2013, Louisiana governor Bobby Jindal warned his fellow Republicans that the time had come for them to stop "being the stupid party" and "insulting the intelligence of voters."

We know. Dream on.

Still, it made a kind of krazee sense, coming from a man who had graduated at age twenty—with honors in two majors—from an Ivy League university; was accepted to Harvard Medical and Yale Law but chose instead to take a master's (poli-sci, emphasis on health policy) at Oxford (the one in *England*) as a Rhodes scholar; was appointed secretary of the Louisiana Department of Health and Hospitals at twenty-four and president of the University of Louisiana System at twenty-eight; worked in health policy for the **Bush Jr.** White House; was elected to Congress at thirty-three; and, at age thirty-six, was elected the youngest governor in the nation. It's beyond impressive. Think of all the twenty-four-year-olds you know. Ask yourself, "How many of those jerks would even know how to *begin* being secretary of the Louisiana Department of Health and Hospitals?"

If Jindal's story had ended on that election day, he'd be remembered as a terrific success: brilliant son (albeit one who converted to Catholicism as a teenager) of Indian immigrants makes good! And somehow manages to convert "Piyush" into "Bobby"! With a straight face!

But his life went on, alas. Many Americans who were not Louisianans first learned of his existence when he delivered the televised GOP response to President Obama's State of the Union address to Congress in February 2009. It was, shall we say, not well received.

Unsurprisingly, Jindal's ideological enemies on the left were less than kind. Rachel Maddow:

> Honestly, the Republican response to Barack Obama's first State of the Union was to invoke government failure during Katrina as a model for how to move forward as a country. I know that I am paid to talk for a living. I am incapable of doing what I am paid to do right now. I am absolutely stunned.

But Jindal's speech was so lame that even Republicans were quick to ridicule him. David Brooks: "To come up at this moment in history with a stale, government-is-the-problem, we can't trust the federal government—it's just a disaster for the Republican Party."

So Jindal faded back into the national wallpaper. And then he popped out again as a 2016 Republican presidential candidate. That's when the public at large began to form an opinion about him. That opinion, which will likely be with him forever, went something like: "OMG! He's a moron!"

Among the things that shaped that opinion, Jindal:

- Despite having been a biology major, passed legislation (the "Louisiana Science Education Act") compelling Louisiana public schools to teach the pseudoscience known as creationism
- Couldn't say whether or not he believes in evolution

- Couldn't say whether he believes in man-made climate change (although he did accuse gay people of causing "a dramatic increase in tornadoes")
- Claimed that "secularized America" is persecuting poor defenseless Christians
- Wrote an op-ed claiming that liberals want to outlaw "religious freedom" by keeping Christian business owners from discriminating against LGBT customers
- Said it was Obama's fault that cops shoot black men, and also blamed Obama for demonstrations in the wake of such shootings
- Signed on to GROVER NORQUIST's tax-cutting Boy Scout Pledge, and drove Louisiana into a totally unnecessary budget crisis
- Called the Obama administration "science deniers" for using established scientific consensus to argue for sensible energy policies

So here's the big question: Is Jindal smart or is he stupid? Or, in some strange quantum superpositional/Heisenbergian sense, is he both at once? Does whichever one he "is" depend on who's looking? In other words: Is "Bobby" Jindal a certified cretin or a cynical scumbag? Or is he really the latter pretending to be the former? But, since it hasn't worked, is he really the former pretending to be the latter *pretending* to be the former?

Wouldn't you love to know how the young Bobby appeared to the Brown admissions board? Wouldn't you love to know what the administrators, professors, students, and alumni of Brown think of Jindal today?

Sure you would! C'mon, Brown. Tell us.

# Theodore Kaczynski

*BA, Harvard University*

Yes, the "Unabomber" — a name concocted by the media from the FBI's designation of the mystery terrorist as UNABOM, for "University and Airline Bomber."

Theodore "Ted" Kaczynski was a brilliant, if awkward, child. He skipped sixth and eleventh grades, easily outstripped his peers (and probably his teachers) in mathematical ability, and entered Harvard at age sixteen. While there he was subjected to an ethically iffy psychology experiment in which students were told they were to discuss their personal beliefs with a fellow student. But, after filling out a form detailing their values and opinions, and having electrodes attached to their heads, the subjects instead were sneeringly grilled and derided by an attorney* and in later phases of the study shown footage of their impotent rage and humiliation. Sound as if it could have helped push socially insecure (and still teenaged) Ted over the line? We don't know.

After Kaczynski graduated, he went to the University of Michigan for his PhD, where his teachers spoke of him in tones of awe. "He was an unusual person," said one of his math professors. "He was not like the other graduate students. He was much more focused about his work. He had a drive to discover mathematical truth." Another said with a sigh, "It is not enough to say he was smart."

---

* The sneeringest type of person there is.

118

Probably. But it is also not enough to say he wasn't in posses-
sion of all his God-given marbles. After he got his PhD he
taught at Berkeley (the youngest professor ever hired, at the
time), but got bad marks from undergrads for mumbling and
being distracted and nervous. He quit soon thereafter, lived
with his parents for two years, and finally moved into a cabin —
kind of a fixer-upper; it lacked electricity and running water —
in the woods near Lincoln, Montana. He did odd jobs, got
money from his family, and briefly worked with his father and
his brother, David (about whom more in a minute), in a foam-
rubber factory. David had to fire Ted for harassing a female
employee.

Kaczynski bought land and built another cabin, determined
to become entirely self-sufficient and to continue his postgrad
studies — sociology and political philosophy — autodidactically.
In the absence of friends, lovers, strangers, colleagues, and
media, his mind became a petri dish for the extravagant prolif-
eration of extreme subjectivity. When, on a hike to his favorite
rural spot, he found it destroyed by a road, he was devastated.
And he wanted revenge.

He was already committing small acts of sabotage against
the encroachments of civilization on his isolated freehold. Now
he began to cultivate a theory — since every miserable, brilliant,
self-taught genius has a theory. His was that civilization had
been on a disastrous track for centuries, reform would never
work to correct it, and only drastic acts of destruction would
awaken the sheeple to their true plight.

So he started mailing bombs. It began in 1978 and lasted
seventeen years, during which time he killed three and
injured twenty-three others. The victims were chosen at random, but all were connected in some way with modern technology. He planted clues about a fictitious insurgent group (FC,

for "Freedom Club") and in all communications referred to himself as "we."*

In 1995, after the third fatality, he sent letters to media outlets saying that if they would publish his 35,000-word manifesto (*Industrial Society and Its Future*), he would cease sending bombs. The ethics, and the wisdom, of printing it was a matter of lively debate, but in the end the *New York Times* and the *Washington Post* ran the screed. In it, Kaczynski expounds an analysis of human history, deploring how most people are driven to depression and despair by the unavailability of meaningful work. (Catchy lede: "...the Industrial Revolution and its consequences have been a disaster for the human race.") Like most theories propounded by intelligent crackpots, it's both somewhat plausible and historically laughable.

The FBI had announced a $1 million reward for information leading to the Unabomber's capture. Once the manifesto was published, the bureau received a thousand calls a day for months — none of which panned out.

But Ted's sister-in-law, Linda, had for a while encouraged David to consider the possibility that the Unabomber was none other than Ted. David had resisted; now he dug out letters and essays Ted had written in the 1970s and saw clear, obvious similarities in his ideas and their expression. David hired an attorney. The attorney hired an investigator. The investigator contacted a former FBI hostage negotiator. Everyone agreed to keep David's name out of it. That failed. Dan Rather told FBI director Louis Freeh he had twenty-four hours to arrest Ted Kaczynski, after which CBS would broadcast the whole story.

FBI agents arrested Kaczynski on April 3, 1996, at his Montana cabin. The evidence — bomb components; reams of journal

---

* We, we should note, also refer to ourselves as "we," but we really *are* we.

pages describing the Unabomber's crimes; a live bomb ready to be shipped — was somewhat* damning. A court-appointed shrink found him to be a paranoid schizophrenic, but still competent to stand trial. To avoid the death penalty Kaczynski pleaded guilty to all federal charges. (At one point he wanted to withdraw the plea, but the judge refused.) He is now serving eight life sentences at a supermaximum security prison in Florence, Colorado.

The minds and personalities of brilliant mathematicians are notoriously fragile.†

---

* A literary device known as "understatement."

† See **Robert Cantor**.

# Gulnara Karimova

*MA, Harvard University*

- She's the glamorous daughter of a dictator, the late* Islam Karimov, president of Uzbekistan!
- She studied jewelry design at the Fashion Institute of Technology in New York and has her own collection with the Swiss jeweler Chopard!
- She has presented her own collection of Uzbek fashions at New York's Fashion Week!
- Under her stage name, Googoosha, she made a music video with Julio Iglesias!
- She made another one with Gérard Depardieu! The song seems loosely based on the iconic 1969 Serge Gainsbourg–Jane Birkin duet *Je t'aime… moi non plus*†: a couple engages in pillow talk (she sings and whispers, he recites) over a lush soundtrack! Mercifully, there is no orgasm finale!
- She wrote an as-yet-unproduced screenplay, to star Depardieu, *The Theft of the White Cocoon,* a period piece set in the fifth and sixth centuries!
- She has her own fragrance lines!‡

---

\* He died in September 2016.

† And its less iconic 1967 predecessor that Gainsbourg recorded with then lover Brigitte Bardot, who asked him to suppress it so as not to infuriate her then husband, Gunter Sachs. Birkin sang and orgasmed an octave higher than Bardot.

‡ Victorious for men, Mysterieuse for women.

- She simultaneously pursued a PhD at the University of World Economy and Diplomacy in Tashkent and a master's in regional studies at Harvard!*
- She was named Uzbekistan's ambassador to Spain in 2010!
- At one time she was the most hated person in Uzbekistan. Several years later — after launching her recording career — she was among the most beloved!
- She was accused of controlling a secretive Swiss-registered conglomerate† with investments in the Uzbek natural resources sector!
- In 2013 she received well over $100 million from a Swedish telecom looking to grease its entry into the Uzbek mobile-phone market! A scandal ensued and her father, the dictator, finally lost patience and placed her under house arrest!
- In 2015 the Organized Crime and Corruption Reporting Project announced that the amount she had received in bribes from Scandinavian and Russian telecoms was upward of $1 billion!
- She has been a target of the United States government's Kleptocracy Asset Recovery Initiative,‡ whose goal is to identify, apprehend, and generally kick the asses of ruling-elite types who have laundered and/or parked and/or conspicuously displayed their illegally gotten gains in the USA!
- She is still, as of this writing, under house arrest in Uzbekistan!

Other than that we have nothing much to say about the multifaceted, unusually well educated Gulnara Karimova!

---

* She evidently has a James Francoesque lust for education.

† Delightfully named Zeromax.

‡ Another entity with a delightful name.

# Henry Kissinger

*BA, Harvard University* ★ *MA, Harvard University*
★ *PhD, Harvard University*

We'll get right to everyone's first question about Henry Kissinger: Is he or is he not a war criminal? The answer is: If he isn't, who is? Herewith, a fractional, partial, pathetically incomplete display of evidence:

### Kissinger Sabotages Vietnam Peace Talks

In 1968, President Johnson was brokering a cease-fire with the North and South Vietnamese governments. He had secretly said he would halt the bombing of North Vietnam on November 1, just before the US presidential election. The governments of both Vietnams appeared to be ready to sign on. Kissinger, a private citizen, not a formal participant in the process, arranged to be in Paris in September while the negotiations were taking place there. With more than a decade of policy wonking at places like the Council on Foreign Relations, the Rockefeller Brothers Fund, the RAND Corporation, and of course various Harvard entities, he knew all the negotiators and wasn't shy about schmoozing with them, talking shop, and offering advice.

Meantime, he was secretly, treacherously, possibly treasonously, leaking what he learned to Richard Nixon, who was running for president against Hubert Humphrey, Johnson's vice president. Though he was polling better than Humphrey, Nixon assumed that good news from the negotiations would be bad news for himself. In an effort to guarantee that there would be no good news from Paris before the election, he got word to Nguyen van Thieu,* South Vietnam's president, that under a Nixon administration his country would get a better deal than he'd get with Humphrey.

Do note that Nixon, like Kissinger, was a private citizen, and that it is a violation of the Logan Act of 1799 — a felony, no less — for a private citizen to poke his nose into negotiations between the US government and a foreign nation. Thieu, of course, didn't give a rat's ass. He reneged on his agreement with LBJ, tanked the talks, and ensured Nixon's election. Recent discoveries at the Richard Nixon Presidential Library suggest — if not prove — that the impetus for this came from Nixon himself. Still, whether this was Kissinger's idea or Nixon's (with Kissinger merely acting as the messenger), the point remains: It violated the law. It prolonged the war for the sake of political gain. And it resulted in the arguably unnecessary deaths of 20,000 American soldiers, the injury of more than 100,000 others, and the deaths or injuries of more than a million Vietnamese.

What was in it for Kissinger? A featured slot in the Nixon administration, first as national security advisor, then as national security advisor *and* secretary of state. It wasn't until just before the *next* presidential election that peace in Vietnam was said to be "at hand"! And, lo, peace miraculously came just as Nixon was reelected.

Here's the totally fucking lovely part. Dr. Henry Kissinger was awarded the Nobel Peace

---

* A known drug- and gunrunner, but hey, nobody's perfect.

Prize* for his part in negotiating the same peace settlement he'd scuttled four years earlier.

## Kissinger Expands War, Is Godfather of Khmer Rouge

The Kissinger-enabled continuation of the Vietnam War led the North Vietnamese forces as well as the South Vietnamese Viet Cong forces to take over regions of eastern Cambodia as staging areas for incursions into South Vietnam; supplies came via the Ho Chi Minh Trail through Laos. Kissinger advised Nixon that it was time to expand the war—illegally, without congressional consent—by carpet-bombing vast swaths of Cambodia and Laos. During the ensuing campaign, Cambodia absorbed 3 million tons of US bombs, significantly more than all the bombs dropped during World War II. Countless thousands of civilians were killed, and out of the chaos rose the Khmer Rouge murder cult, which was responsible for another 1.5 to 3 million deaths.

By the way, if you're keeping score at home, be sure to make note of the facts that a) Kissinger's grand military and diplomatic strategies were failures—the US lost the war; b) his geopolitical theorizing was incompetent: "all of Southeast Asia" did not go communist; c) the few countries that did (Vietnam, Cambodia, Laos) were hostile to one another and represented the opposite of an "international communist conspiracy"; and, of course, d) all eventually became capitalist societies anyway.

## And More

Then there was the time, in 1971, when Bangladesh broke away from Pakistan, and Pakistan retaliated by sending in troops to

---

* In an unprecedented move, two members of the Nobel Committee resigned in protest.

mass-rape Hindu women and kill as many Hindus as possible. There were up to 3 million murders and 400,000 rapes. Kissinger's response was to recall the US ambassador, who was begging the administration to intervene. Kissinger also sent a note to the Pakistani dictator who had ordered the butchery, commending him for his "delicacy and tact."

And don't forget the Kissinger-engineered CIA coup in Chile, which, in 1973, replaced the democratically elected socialist Salvador Allende with fascist strongman Augusto Pinochet. (See the **William F. Buckley** entry for a taste of Pinochet's depravities.) In 1975, meeting with the Chilean foreign minister, Kissinger displayed his legendary wit by ridiculing his own staffers for having put human rights on the agenda. "I read the briefing paper for this meeting," he said, "and it was nothing but human rights. The State Department is made up of people who have a vocation for the ministry. Because there are not enough churches for them, they went into the Department of State." The man is hilarious!

We concede that some of Kissinger's actions might not have risen to the level of "war criminal." Does selling out the Kurds to appease Saddam Hussein rise to that level? Does supporting Indonesian president and epic embezzler Suharto's invasion of East Timor rise to that level? You make the call. Or we can keep going. There's lots more where that came from.

# William Kristol

*BA, Harvard University ★ PhD, Harvard University*
*★ University of Pennsylvania Faculty ★ Harvard University*
*Faculty*

*I remember back in the late 1990s, when Ira Katznelson, an eminent political scientist at Columbia, came to deliver a guest lecture. Prof. Katznelson described a lunch he had with Irving Kristol during the first Bush administration.*

*The talk turned to William Kristol, then Dan Quayle's chief of staff, and how he got his start in politics.*

*Irving recalled how he talked to his friend Harvey Mansfield at Harvard, who secured William a place there as both an undergrad and graduate student; how he talked to Pat Moynihan, then Nixon's domestic policy adviser, and got William an internship at the White House; how he talked to friends at the RNC [Republican National Committee] and secured a job for William after he got his Harvard PhD; and how he arranged with still more friends for William to teach at Penn and the Kennedy School of Government.*

*With that, Prof. Katznelson recalled, he then asked Irving what he thought of affirmative action. "I oppose it," Irving replied. "It subverts meritocracy."*

— *The Daily Dish* blog, *The Atlantic*, 9/19/09

William "Bill" Kristol is the son of Irving Kristol, a heavyweight postwar intellectual who started as an anti-Stalinist Trotskyite and, as did many disillusioned with the Soviet Union and burdened with a Manichean outlook, eventually went nuts and fell in with the Republican right. During his first year in grad school, Bill roomed with conservative black person and certifiable lunatic Alan Keyes and acted as campaign manager for Keyes's unsuccessful 1988 Maryland senatorial campaign vs. the nice, liberal, sane Paul Sarbanes.

With Keyes, Kristol began one third of his career, i.e., the promoting and championing of idiots for high political office. After taking a few years off—teaching, working as chief of staff for Secretary of Education William Bennett (who wrote *The Book of Virtues* while nursing is gambling addiction)—he resumed promoting nudniks and became staff chief for Vice President Dan Quayle, which prompted *The New Republic* to bestow on Kristol the faint-praise epithet "Quayle's Brain." The high point of the Quayle–Kristol mind meld came when Quayle and/or his "brain" decided to deplore American culture by criticizing the fictional TV character Murphy Brown, and as so often happens in sitcoms, hilarity ensued.

Kristol's masterpiece of idiot-impresarioship, however, would wait until 2007. In June of that year, Kristol and fellow putz Fred Barnes had lunch with Governor Sarah Palin of Alaska, and the fellas fell in love. Palin took it from there, commencing her transformation from little-known weird-state chief executive, to openly ignorant campaigner, to shrill demagogue, to what we see today, a batshit lady playing the Muppet version of "Sarah Palin."

We jump back to 1992, when Quayle and his boss, PRESIDENT GEORGE H. W. BUSH, lost to **Bill Clinton** and **Al Gore,** and Kristol moved on. In 1994, with fellow neocon nepotism beneficiary John Podhoretz, he founded *The Weekly Standard.* He also chaired or directed this or that "project," culminating in the creation of the Project for the New American Century in 1997. This would jump-start the second third of Kristol's career:

the serious, grave, patriotic, wrongheaded, mendacious promotion of the invasion of Iraq.

By then, both as editor of the *Standard* and as a frequent guest on TV chat shows, Bill had already commenced the third third of his career, one that has eclipsed even his moron-championing: making confident, utterly wrong political predictions. A brief, by-no-means-exhaustive, timeline of his failed prognostications would include these gems:

- April 1993: An upcoming march in Washington will be "the high water mark" of the gay- and lesbian-rights movement.
- September 2002: The war in Iraq "could have terrifically good effects throughout the Middle East."
- November 2002: Removing Saddam Hussein "would start a chain reaction in the Arab world that would be very healthy."
- February 2003: "If we free the people of Iraq, we will be respected in the Arab world...and I think we will be respected around the world."
- March 2003: The Iraq war will last two months, with little chance of sectarian conflict afterward; "Very few wars in American history were prepared better or more thoroughly than this one by this president"; "We'll be vindicated when we discover the weapons of mass destruction"; the war will cost $100–$200 billion (actual cost: north of $2 *trillion*).
- April 2003: The battles of Afghanistan and Iraq will be seen as having been won "decisively and honorably."
- December 2006: Hillary Clinton will prevail in the Democratic primaries over Barack Obama.
- November 2008: Ted Stevens will defeat Mark Begich in Alaska's Senate race; he didn't.

- May 2009: Barack Obama will name Michigan governor Jennifer Granholm to the US Supreme Court; he named Sonia Sotomayor.
- June 2011: Rudy Giuliani will be the 2012 Republican nominee for president.
- Anytime after June 2015: People are tired of the Republican frontrunner and have reached "Peak Trump"—a prediction he made, and had to remake, more than *ten times* during Trump's run for the GOP nomination.
- October 2015: Joe Biden will enter the race for the Democratic nomination for president.
- February 2016: Marco Rubio will win the New Hampshire primary; guess who didn't win the New Hampshire primary.

The list, as they say, goes on and on. He was right about one thing, though. In an editorial in the *Standard* published in March 2003, Kristol wrote about the US's invasion of Iraq: "The war itself will clarify who was right and who was wrong about weapons of mass destruction." Indeedy.

Does it matter that he's always—okay, infinitesimally close to always—wrong? Who, after all, can really predict the future?

The thing is, "predicting the future" is the pundit's *job*. If a stock picker, an astrologist, or a gypsy fortuneteller failed in his or her predictions as much and as publicly as Bill Kristol, he or she would be drummed out of the profession. But punditry—especially on the Republican side—is the world's least accountable profession, and Kristol is the world's most inept, least accountable pundit.

How's *that* for subverting meritocracy, Pops?

# Arthur Laffer

*BA, Yale University* ★ *MBA, Yale University*

Cast your mind back to 1974, when Arthur Laffer (who holds a PhD in economics from Stanford, yes, but also a BA and an MBA from Yale) was meeting with DICK CHENEY and DONALD RUMSFELD as well as with right-wing journalist and economics chatterer Jude Wanniski. Laffer grabbed a napkin and drew on it a graph showing how government revenue, which would of course be zero when tax rates were either 0 percent or 100 percent, rose to a certain height and then *dropped,* as a function of increasing tax rates. There was, therefore, an ideal level of taxation below which government revenue would fall short, but above which economic health and vigor would be compromised.

Yes, workers who don't have enough money, because they're overtaxed, would work *less.* Workers taxed less, and keeping more, would work *more.* Make sense?

No, but imagine the delight of Darth and Rummy. Everyone gazing at the napkin agreed: tax rates at the time — especially on the wealthy — were too high. If only someone would lower them to Laffer's ideal level! Then, the "theory" went, workers would work more, expanding the economy, generating more tax revenues, and maximizing the whole schmeer.

The graph became known as "the Laffer curve" (so named by Wanniski) and formed the intellectual basis — such as it was — for "supply-side economics." Laffer modestly allowed as how the idea wasn't original to him — he had learned it from the fourteenth-century North African Arab historian Ibn Khaldun (full name: Abdurahman bin Muhammad bin Muhammad bin Muhammad bin Al-Hasan bin Jabir bin Muhammad bin Ibrahim bin Abdurahman bin Ibn Khaldun) and noted economist John Maynard Keynes. Still, they were dead. And Laffer was alive! Alive, we tell you! And thus able to inspire also-fairly-alive Ronald Reagan when he came to office six years later, laying the theoretical groundwork for the economic boom that followed, until it didn't.

(We'd like to pause here and note that, for all the good and bad things about his presidency, GEORGE H. W. BUSH has never received adequate credit for calling Laffer's folly "voodoo economics." It struck us then, as it does now, as a better description than people know. Voodoo, as people do know, is a syncretic religion in which, among other things, effects are visited upon people, for good or ill, via the propitiation of various gods, and the symbolic acts visited upon physical representations of the target — e g , you obtain a lock of hair of the beloved or behated person, do stuff to it, appeal to Ogun or Whomever with cigars and rum and chicken bones, and — magically — the subject of your concern experiences actual consequences. Same with supply-side economics: Lower taxes and people, spurred by being allowed to keep more of what they earn, will, like propitiated gods, "work more" or "work harder," expanding the economy and generating an increase in government revenue. Thus, "voodoo."* Well said, Poppy.)

---

* Or here's another way to think about it: Lower income and capital gains taxes and make goods and services more available — increase output on the "supply side" — and consumers will be affected the way the cheating-lover subject of a voodoo ceremony will experience pain when his doll effigy is stabbed by the *houngans* and *mambos* (male and female priests). It's spooky action at a distance, capitalism-style. They'll experience sudden, inexplicable urges. They'll buy! Buy! Buy! The economy will expand, and the government — even at the lower tax rates — will see increased revenue.

Does it work? No. It's magical thinking, silly. Like voodoo.

It didn't work out that way. Even many conservative economists said that supply-side gains didn't generate enough revenue to offset Reagan's tax cuts. As for nonconservative
economists, we give you Paul Krugman:

> Since the 1970s there have been four big changes in the
> effective tax rate on the top 1 percent: the Reagan cut,
> the Clinton hike, the Bush cut, and the Obama hike.
> Republicans are fixated on the boom that followed the
> 1981 tax cut (which had much more to do with monetary
> policy, but never mind). But they predicted dire effects
> from the Clinton hike; instead we had a boom that
> eclipsed Reagan's. They predicted wonderful things from
> the Bush tax cuts; instead we got an unimpressive expan-
> sion followed by a devastating crash. And they predicted
> terrible things from the tax rise after Obama's reelection;
> instead we got the best job growth since 1999.

So thanks for nothing, Arthur Laffer, who, Krugman also
notes,

> ...has a truly extraordinary record of being wrong at
> crucial turning points....Laffer was even wrong during
> the Reagan years: he predicted that the Reagan tax hikes
> of 1982, which partially reversed earlier cuts, would crip-
> ple the economy; "morning in America" promptly fol-
> lowed. Oh, and let's not forget his 2009 warnings about
> soaring interest rates and inflation.

Maybe next time we try stimulating the economy with tax
cuts, we'll know enough to add cigars, rum, and chicken bones.

# Harry H. Laughlin

*DSc, Princeton University*

Credit where credit is due: Harry Laughlin did not invent the idea of sterilizing "undesirables" to improve the human gene pool. He just provided an authoritative pseudoscientific framework for it, then labored strenuously to see sterilization laws enacted across the country and around the world. No, he didn't invent it, but you had to admit it: sterilization was his shtick.

He was a latecomer to eugenics. Born and educated in the Iowa boonies, he became a schoolteacher, then a principal, then a school-superintendent cum-teacher-of-future-farmers. An interest in breeding animals evolved, naturally enough, into an interest in breeding human beings, which led him, in 1907, at the somewhat advanced age of twenty-seven, to contact leading human-breeding theorist **Charles Davenport,** founder of the Station for Experimental Evolution, and its devil-spawn, the Eugenics Records Office at the Cold Spring Harbor Laboratory on Long Island. Laughlin must have been a hell of a letter writer, at least when it came to letters about eugenics: Davenport invited him to come east and run the Records Office.

Eugenics remained Laughlin's calling for the rest of his life. Somehow he found the time to pick up a DSc — equivalent to a PhD of today — from Princeton in cytology, or cell biology, when he was thirty-seven. This conferred a measure of magisterial authority on his "findings." And it surely helped pave the way toward the honorary degree the University of Heidelberg bestowed upon him in 1936. Hmm. That place and time rings a bell. What was going on in Germany in 1936?

But we're jumping ahead of ourselves. Twelve American states had compulsory sterilization laws on the books before Laughlin came along, but few states had the stomach to enforce them. Laughlin wanted to fix this. His work involved, among other things, producing a prodigious amount of writing on eugenics, sterilization, immigration, and the promotion of eugenics through the sterilization of immigrants. His chef d'oeuvre, the snappily titled *Eugenical Sterilization in the United States* (Psychopathic Laboratory of the Municipal Court of Chicago,* 1922), established him as a star in his field. By producing what passed for statistical proof that certain groups of people were simply "unfit" to reproduce—and by crafting an example of a law for compulsory sterilization†—he empowered another twelve states to pass enforceable sterilization laws.

Virginia passed a eugenics law in 1924 and cracked down posthaste. The first person up for sterilization—a woman characterized by the state as the "probable potential parent of socially inadequate offspring"‡—naturally sued. Colleagues of Laughlin testified against her, and Laughlin himself, who never met her, presented a deposition asserting that she belonged to "the shiftless, ignorant, and worthless class of anti-social whites of the South." The state won, the case went to the Supreme Court, the court went with Laughlin, and the woman was sterilized. She was one of more than 60,000 citizens of the US who were

---

* You can't make this shit up.

† Who(m) did he want to sterilize? The "feeble-minded" and insane; alcoholics and criminals; epileptics; the blind; the deaf; the deformed; the poor; and, probably, you.

‡ You can't make this shit up.

rendered incapable of reproducing over the course of the sterilization craze, which lasted into the 1970s. *The 1970s!*

Dr. Laughlin, we should add, also had a hand in the criminalization of miscegenation. And in restricting the flow of immigrants from southern and eastern Europe (because they were considered far more likely to be "socially inadequate" than the fine people of northern and western Europe). And we'd be shirking our responsibility if we didn't mention that he wrote "a eugenical comedy in four acts" for the entertainment of his coworkers. And that his sterilization laws attracted a worldwide audience.

Which brings us back to Germany.

In 1933 the Nazi party, in one of its first legislative actions, passed the Law for the Prevention of Hereditarily Diseased Offspring.* It was based on Laughlin's pioneering legal model, imported from the US along with the racist fake science of **William Z. Ripley** and **Madison Grant**. The Nazis sterilized more than 350,000 people over the twelve years of their reign, which must have made Laughlin's heart-cockles feel nice and toasty. And that honorary University of Heidelberg degree for his epic work on the "science of racial cleansing": icing on the *sachertorte.*

But as details of Nazi lunacy filtered into the American media mainstream, it became apparent that improving the gene pool, racial cleansing, racial hygiene, sterilization, whatever you call it, was not as well loved by the American public as it was by the nation's small cadre of highly placed racists. Support for this branch of putative scientific research plummeted, and by 1939 funding had dried up and the Eugenics Records Office was no more.

---

* You can't…oh, never mind.

One last note. In his spare time, Harry Laughlin devoted considerable energy to thinking about, writing about, and agitating for the establishment of a world government. The primary goal: to prevent the intermixing of the races. Naturally, in his vision he and like-minded Ivy-bred technocrats were to be in charge of the world.

# Cardinal Bernard Francis Law

*BA, Harvard University*

If you've seen the movie *Spotlight,* winner of the 2015 Academy Award for Best Picture, you know the story of the vast child-molestation scandal that was covered up for years by the Catholic archdiocese of Boston. And you know that the former archbishop of Boston, Bernard Francis Law (played by Len Cariou), was actively involved in concealing the sexual predations of dozens if not hundreds of priests.

Law was an air force brat, which meant an itinerant childhood: born in Mexico, he attended schools in various US states and Colombia before graduating from high school in the Virgin Islands. He did well enough to get into Harvard, where he majored in medieval history. After graduating in 1953, he segued to the medieval setting of the Catholic Church, doing graduate work at a seminary in Louisiana and another in Ohio. He was ordained in 1961.

His first priestly gig was in Mississippi. Given the way this story ends, it may surprise you to learn that, in the Deep South in the 1960s, Father Law blossomed into an outspoken civil rights advocate. As in, riling up the racists so badly that he received death threats. As in, being publicly praised by Charles Evers, brother of the slain civil rights activist Medgar Evers.

Law's civil rights work turned him into a

star. He ascended to bishop in the early 1970s and was tapped by the Vatican to work on various nontraditional issues, such as forging a better relationship with the Jews and figuring out how to import Episcopalian priests (even married ones) into the Roman Catholic hierarchy. In 1984 he hit the big time: archbishop of Boston and then, the following year, cardinal!

As we all now know, one problem with being a capo in the Catholic Church is that you've got so damned many depraved child molesters working for you. And, at least if you're Cardinal Law, and your interests have evolved from defending the down-trodden to protecting the Church, you can't just fire them and report them to the civil authorities. No, what you do, if you're Cardinal Law, is when you learn that a priest has done unthink-able things to a child, you quietly move that priest to another diocese. This provides some relief for your parishioners, an out-of-sight, out-of-mind relief to you, and — although you pre-tend you don't know this — fresh meat for the pervy priest.

One example. Father John Geoghan was accused of impos-ing himself on more than 130 children. Law knew all about it but did not call the police. Instead, the cardinal moved him to a new parish each time a parental outcry threatened to blast through the Church's wall of *omertà*. Eventually even Law couldn't contain the news of Geoghan's rampant pederasty, and in 2002 the priest was arrested, convicted, and sentenced to prison.*

Multiply Geoghan by more than 200 rogue priests, with more than 500 known victims, and you'll begin to understand the breadth of the problem. And the egregiousness of Law's cover-up. And the importance of the *Boston Globe*'s Spotlight

---

* Where, less than a year later, he was murdered by his cellmate, who was an even nastier predator than Geoghan.

reporting. And the consequent ruin the Church brought down upon itself, both to its global brand and its financial stability.*

Bernard Law resigned as archbishop of Boston in late 2002, but he remained Cardinal Law and, for some reason, was not subject to prosecution. Soon he'd procured a big-time sinecure at the Vatican itself, no doubt as a token of gratitude for his loyalty and as an indication of the opinion of many other cardinals that Law was the victim of a witch-hunt rather than an enabler of criminal behavior and destroyer of children.

In his final years on earth, we imagine that Bernard Law has plenty of time to reflect upon his life. And we'd like to think that, with his Harvard-honed knowledge of medieval history, he carries within him a vivid, haunting, and relentless vision of what awaits him in the eternal damnation of the Roman Catholic hell.

---

* As we type, the Church is still negotiating a settlement with the victims and their families. It is currently hovering at around $65 million.

# Jonah Lehrer

*BA, Columbia University*

Jonah Lehrer was fast out of the gate. He studied neuroscience at Columbia, where for two years he was editor of the *Columbia Review*. After that, he was a 2003 Rhodes Scholar, and went to Wolfson College at Oxford, and th—

Hold on. Go back. What *is* the *Columbia Review*? Why, it's the country's oldest college literary magazine. And maybe that should have been a signal of the fictionalizing and creative writing to come.

Returning to the US, Lehrer decided he didn't have what it took for a career in science. So he began a career as an explainer of science. And he was great at it. His first book, *Proust Was a Neuroscientist,* was a series of essays about famous people, published by the prestigious publishing house of Houghton Mifflin in 2007. Sure, it was smacked around by real scientists. But nonscientists lavished it with praise, and it became a best-seller.

Soon Lehrer was publishing in *The New Yorker, Wired, Scientific American Mind, Nature,* and other magazines. His specialty was neuroscience for the educated masses. And, since neuroscience was (and still is) *the* hot topic in psychological circles, Lehrer had carte blanche to write about any damn thing he wanted. He was good on radio. He was good on the lecture circuit. He was young, adorable, and happening. His next book, *How We Decide,* came out in 2009. It, too, became a best-seller.

Then, in 2012, writers for *New York* magazine and *Slate* discovered that Lehrer pieces often featured not just sentences but whole paragraphs that had been published elsewhere — by Jonah Lehrer. Yes, he was "self-plagiarizing" — or, to put it more delicately, "recycling" his material.

Is that so very wrong? Thriftily reusing writing that's already yours, the better to keep up with a high-demand career? Well, it's not illegal. But it is sort of cheat-y, especially to the magazines and websites that think they're buying original writing, in order to please and delight their readers, who also think *they're* being given original writing. Call it unethical. Still, there are worse writerly crimes. Like, e.g., transplanting text from press releases and calling it your own. And actually plagiarizing material from other people's work. And conflating, misstating, or outright inventing quotations.

Lehrer was discovered to have been guilty of all these literary felonies. In March of 2012, Houghton published his *Imagine: How Creativity Works*. It was another best-seller. But Michael C. Moynihan, a reporter and an avid Bob Dylan fan, noticed something amiss in the book's chapter on Dylan. The quotes didn't sound right. And the more Moynihan pressed Lehrer for sourcing and confirmation, the more he got a runaround, evasions, contradictory explanations, and the like.

Moynihan published a damning piece in *Tablet* in late July 2012 detailing the whole story. When (four years later) he was interviewed by Matt Welch of *Reason*'s blog *Hit and Run*, Moynihan said that once Lehrer was caught having lied, he went off the record "to lie and lie and lie and lie to me these fantastical, brilliantly spun lies that I could never talk about. And I have never talked about them, because they were off the record."

Then things got worse. Wired.com recruited journalism professor Charles Seife to examine Lehrer's online oeuvre — and of the eighteen representative pieces Seife reviewed, seventeen had problems. Fourteen featured "recycling" of previous material.

Five contained "press-release plagiarism." Three contained outright plagiarism. Four had "quotation issues" and four had "factual issues."

Houghton pulled *Imagine*. It decided that *Proust* was clean, but the publisher also pulled *How We Decide*. Lehrer resigned his staff position at *The New Yorker*. Wired.com bid him farewell, too.

In February 2013, Lehrer gave a well-covered "apology speech" to the John S. and James L. Knight Foundation. The fact that the foundation paid Lehrer $20,000 for it did not go over well, and neither did the speech. *Slate* said it was "couched in elaborate and perplexing disavowals." The *Times* said, "As apologies go, it was both arrogant and pathetic." Noting which way the wind was blowing, Lehrer retired from the public eye.

This monster movie, like many of a previous era, could conclude here with *The End*...? But it's not quite over. In 2016 Lehrer published a book about love entitled *A Book About Love* (Simon and Schuster). The ink was barely dry when Jennifer Senior gave it the back of her hand in the *New York Times*. She criticized its content ("This book is a series of duckpin arguments, just waiting to be knocked down"). And while she mentions Lehrer's introductory avowals that he sent his quotes to everyone he interviewed and had the manuscript independently fact-checked, still...

I fear Mr. Lehrer has simply become more artful about his appropriations. At one point, for instance, he writes: "We don't love our kids despite their demands; we love them because of them. Caregiving makes us care."

I stopped dead when I read that sentence. Reread it. And read it again. It sounds to me like a clever adaptation of one of the most beautiful lines in *The Philosophical*

*Baby* by Alison Gopnik: "It's not so much that we care for children because we love them as that we love them because we care for them."

I'm pretty certain Mr. Lehrer read Ms. Gopnik's quote. Why? Because I cite it in my own book—which he cites, twice. (Though not for that.)

To coin a phrase: Fool me once, shame on you. Fool me... you can't get fooled again.*

---

* Do you see what we did there? We claimed, or at least implied, we were feeding you an original line ("coined"), then slipped you someone else's line (and a really stupid one, originally uttered by stumblebrained monster **George W. Bush**), thus not only illustrating but *demonstrating* the type of wrongdoing committed by the present profilee.

# Joe Lieberman

*BA, Yale University ★ JD, Yale University*

Here's all you really need to know about Joe Lieberman. In 2008, while he was a Democratic senator from Connecticut, he endorsed the Republican candidate, John McCain, for president. (John McCain. *You* know—the guy who selected as his running mate that wildly unqualified, babbling idiot, Sarah Palin.) McCain, you'll recall, was running against Barack Obama, who was not only the candidate of Lieberman's own party but who had a running mate who was, more often than not, coherent. Lieberman, drippingly serious as always, announced that he had made his principled choice based on McCain's tough stance on terrorism. Or was it really because McCain had teased him with a shot at being vice president

before he chose the Alaskan grifter? Or because, after that, he teased him with a chance of being secretary of state in the McCain administration?

What we know is that Lieberman continued to support McCain even after it became obvious that McCain contained only trace elements of the Presidential Right Stuff, and that Sarah Palin was full-to-bursting with dumbbell bullshit.

Let's stop here. Except, no, let's not stop here. Instead, let's review some optional things to know about Joe Lieberman:

- He was the first Democratic senator to join the Republicans in condemning **Bill Clinton** for being the recipient of a non-spousal blow job in the White House.
- He was a leading advocate for **George W. Bush**'s stupid, pointless, lethal, expensive, lie-based invasion of Iraq in 2003.
- He wanted the federal government to have more surveillance cameras to spy on, you know, *us*.
- He wanted to make it more difficult to investigate the government's use of illegal wiretaps. Do you see a theme here?
- He avidly supported the confirmation, in 2006, of Sam Fox as George W. Bush's ambassador to Belgium. Fox, a rich guy and big GOP donor, had contributed $50,000 to the Swift Boat Veterans for Truth, a group whose sole purpose was to help Bush get reelected in 2004 by spreading vicious lies about Democrat John Kerry's Vietnam service.[*]
- During his next senate campaign, two years later, he took money from Sam Fox.
- When one vote was needed to pass the "public option" piece of the Affordable Care Act, he voted against it.
- After he retired from the Senate, he joined the conservative American Enterprise Institute alongside many of the neocons responsible for the glories of the George W. Bush administration.

Having experienced a presidential race up close and personal as **Al Gore**'s running mate in the 2000 election, Lieberman decided to give it a go himself as a Democratic candidate in 2004. It is a credit to the American people that he did extremely

---

[*] The sick part is that Kerry actually fought in the war while Bush was AWOL from the Texas Air National Guard, doing who knows what.

poorly in the Democratic primaries of 2003. Not only did he fail to get the support of Gore, he didn't seem to have the support of anyone. He won not a single primary or caucus and finished dead last of the seven candidates, behind even Dennis Kucinich, General Wesley Clark, and Reverend Al Sharpton.

He ascribed his unpopularity to his support for the war in Iraq, but we think he was flattering himself.

Okay, *now* we're done.

# Nathan Lord

*Dartmouth College President*

Nathan Lord, born in 1793 in Berwick, Maine, had a mother whose first, or "Christian," name was Mehitable. The all-knowing Internet tells us that Mehitable is a biblical name, which sets the tone for our Nathan Lord story. Come to think of it, so does Lord.

Nathan Lord graduated from Bowdoin College at sixteen, taught for a while at Phillips Exeter Academy,* studied theology, and became a preacher in Amherst, New Hampshire. He also became a trustee of Dartmouth College, about eighty miles to the northwest. After a throat ailment put an end to his preaching career, he was elected president of Dartmouth, in 1828.

To all who knew him, Nathan Lord was a model of piety, a fine Christian, a true believer in the sense that he believed that the Bible was the direct, faultless word of God. He was also the only college president in New England to be an out-of-the closet abolitionist, and in 1833 was elected vice president of the American Anti-Slavery Society.

But then a funny thing happened, and we don't mean funny ha-ha. A fellow abolitionist pointed out that the Bible not only condones slavery, it even stipulates a set of rules for how slaves should be treated. Said the fellow abolitionist to Lord—and

---

* We'd like to see some seventeen-year-old smarty-pants teenager try to teach there today.

we'll take the liberty of modernizing his speech—"If it's between the Bible and antislavery, I'll take antislavery."

This blew poor Lord's mind. It never occurred to him that the Bible wasn't, you know, dictated by God, or however that was supposed to work, and perfect in every particular. So he embarked on a period of intense Bible study to see what he could discover re: slavery. What he discovered was that slavery is just dandy, as long as you approach it with proper biblical etiquette.* And so Lord, True Believer that he was, "pivoted" on slavery. It was now, he concluded, a Good Thing as long as it was executed according to biblical precepts. Which meant that you shouldn't be *mean* to them. Which meant that you could buy and sell them, separate families, force them to work from dawn to dusk for zero compensation, and condescend to them until the cows came home, and then force them to tend to the cows. As long as you weren't mean to them.

He then wrote a thirty-five-page letter, broadcast to others of his ilk—which is to say, ministers of the Gospel—explaining that he'd changed his mind: slavery's cool, slavery's good for the slaves, disregard previous deeply held conviction. His ilk promptly wrote or yelled back that he was full of shit. He then wrote another letter, conceding that the current version of slavery *was* pretty bad, but the ideal biblical version was really nice, especially for the Negroes, whom slavery helps by disciplining and Christianizing them. Do note that, other than wishing to enslave them, Lord had no particular grievance with black people; he went so far as to admit them to Dartmouth, the only such institution at the time to do so.

Then, in 1863, he went and blocked Dartmouth's board of

---

* Point to ponder: If he was such a learned preacherman, why did someone else have to point out that slavery was A-OK with the Bible? Had he never read the whole thing before?

trustees from presenting an honorary degree to the antislavery president of the USA, Abraham Lincoln. This was especially foolish, as Amos Tuck, a powerful Dartmouth trustee,* was not only the founder of the Republican Party but a close friend of Lincoln's. After meeting to discuss the Lincoln fiasco, the trustees and faculty issued a statement that was in effect a vote of no confidence in Lord, who promptly resigned.†

The Civil War ended in 1865. As you may know, the antislavery side won. Nathan Lord died in 1870, which gave him five years to ponder what it means when the proslavery Lord of the Bible (never mind the proslavery Lord of Dartmouth) gets His supernatural Ass overruled so dramatically.

---

* And eponym of Dartmouth's business school.

† Although he surely thought he was right and they were wrong. After all: the Bible.

# Abbott Lawrence Lowell

*BA, Harvard University ★ LLB, Harvard University*
*★ Harvard University President*

He could have been genetically engineered to be president of Harvard: born into a family of aristocratic Boston Brahmins; paternal grandfather a longtime member of the Harvard Corporation; maternal grandfather founder of the Lawrence Scientific School at Harvard; father a Harvard alum. Of course he went there too, got a BA and a law degree, and taught there after practicing law for a while with his cousin Francis Cabot Lowell, who also had a pair of Harvard degrees.

Which isn't to say that Lawrence Lowell adored everything about his alma mater. When he was named president, in 1909, he was deeply offended by the class divisions, the way the rich kids tended to live in fancy off-campus housing while others lived in the decrepit student housing in Harvard Yard. And he didn't care for the well-off students' lazy disdain for classwork and their infernal gentleman's Cs.* He quickly whipped the place into shape, raising funds to build new dorms and requiring all freshmen to dwell therein to promote a "democratic social life." He revamped the curriculum, introducing the concept of the concentration or major, which forced students to actually study and gain knowledge rather than skate by with the easiest classes available every semester. And he cast a wider admissions

---

\* See **George W. Bush,** lest you think the Ivies eradicated this in the early 1900s.

net, seeking top candidates from schools that did not typically send their graduates to Harvard.

He was, in short, a progressive, and progress was definitely achieved during his twenty-four-year tenure as president. However, as with many progressives of his generation (see **Charles Davenport, Madison Grant, Harry Laughlin,** and **William Z. Ripley**), Lowell's idea of progress had a strong component of narcissism, or outright prejudice: progress meant Making the World a Better Place for Me and People Like Me. Which inevitably had a flip side: Making the World a Worse Place for People Who Are Not Like Me. And Lowell definitely made the world worse for three types of students who were Not Like Him.

We'll pause while you guess which three kinds of students suffered Lowell's disapprobation. Got it? Okay.

In May 1920, a Harvard student named Cyril Wilcox confessed to his big brother, George, that he was sexually involved with an older man. The next day Cyril killed himself. In quick succession the furious, grieving George found letters to Cyril from two other gay Harvard students, tracked down the older man and beat him until he gave up the names of others involved with his brother, and accosted a dean of the school to demand that Harvard homosexuals be exposed and destroyed.

With Lowell's blessing, the dean convened a so-called Secret Court to track down the hated (and feared) gay men and administer justice. Ultimately, eight students were expelled (one of whom killed himself the month after Cyril Wilcox's suicide), an assistant professor was fired, and a recent graduate was proclaimed persona non grata. Parents were informed, and the expelled students were essentially blacklisted from attending college elsewhere, as Harvard was brutal when responding to transcript requests.* Lowell initially opposed any gesture of clemency, but he eventually allowed two of the expelled students to complete their studies.

Would you care to guess who else Wasn't Like Lowell? If you said "the blacks," you're right, and we appreciate your **Donald Trump** impersonation. Starting in 1915, per Lowell's mandate, all first-year students were to live in campus housing reserved for freshmen. All, that is, except for black freshmen, who Lowell felt should live...someplace else.† "We owe to the colored man," he wrote, "the same opportunities for education that we do to the white man; but we do not owe it to him to force him and the white into social relations that are not, or may not be, mutually congenial." To the credit of the Harvard community, an outpouring of protest in 1922 — mainly by students, but also by faculty and alumni — led the Board of Overseers to review the situation. Lowell disingenuously argued that the effect of forcing blacks and whites to live together would be to increase the amount of prejudice against blacks.‡ The Board of Overseers responded wisely by unanimously rejecting Lowell's segregation policy.

And then — surprise! — there was Lowell's Jewish problem. (Did you guess all three? Good job!) At the outset of his presidency, the Jewish population of Harvard was 6 percent. By 1925, after Lowell's meritocratic admissions policies had been

---

* The schools on the receiving end were universally thankful to Harvard for tipping them off about the transfer applicants' depravity.

† Which was especially odd since black and white students had been living peacefully together in Harvard dorms for years before Lowell instituted his new "democratic" policy.

‡ You have to admire the gall of this sort of racist jiujitsu. It's like saying, "Of course the races are equal. So we must keep them separate, so that blacks aren't oppressed by people who think they're *not* equal, having had no experience with them because we've been keeping them separate."

in place for a decade and a half, it had risen to 28 percent. This, for his taste, was far too high. His argument for reducing the number of incoming Jews was related to his argument for segregating the freshman dorms: the presence of so many Jews at Harvard was causing an uptick in anti-Semitism, which was bad for the Jewish students, ergo there should be fewer of them. He then undermined the argument by suggesting that Harvard might suffer the same fate as certain elite clubs who see a decline in their traditional membership when they admit too many Jews.*

None of this sat well with the faculty or the Overseers, but Lowell persisted in his effort to fine-tune and tweak and hone and rejigger the admissions process until he was satisfied that it was functioning properly. And he succeeded. By the time he stepped down in 1933, he had reduced the proportion of Jews in the incoming freshman class to a safe, manageable, and less offensive 10 percent. Just *enough* Jews. Just *enough* anti-Semitism.

---

* I.e., "Too many Jews leads to more anti-Semitism. Plus, it alienates anti-Semites, so they don't come to Harvard, resulting in *less* anti-Semitism, which is also, for some reason, bad."

# Sean Ludwick

*MA, University of Pennsylvania ★ MBA, University of Pennsylvania (Wharton)*

Sean Ludwick, a wealthy forty-two-year-old New York City real estate developer, was staying at his house in Bridgehampton. It was a Saturday night in August 2015. Ludwick went out drinking in Southampton with Paul Hansen, fifty-two, a Hamptons-based Douglas Elliman real estate agent. What Hansen, a devoted family man, was doing with Ludwick, a dedicated womanizer and well-known lowlife,* is anyone's guess.† Developing a potential client? Ludwick drank a lot of tequila and hit on a blond Morgan Stanley financial advisor. In the wee hours of Sunday morning, he gave up his quest, stumbled out of the bar, and got behind the wheel of his silver 2013 Porsche Carrera convertible. The idea was, he would take Hansen home to Sag Harbor, pick up his eleven-year-old son, who was having a sleepover at the Hansens', then drive himself and the kid back to Bridgehampton.

It was a reasonable plan, but the execution was flawed: Ludwick crashed at high speed into a utility pole in front of Han-

---

* Does a 2014 arrest for breaking into an ex-girlfriend's apartment and scribbling penises on murals that he himself had painted, then sending obscene messages from her e-mail account to execs at her company, merit the insult? We think so. And we haven't even mentioned his previous DWI. Or the time he smacked a girlfriend, tore the phone off the wall so she couldn't call 911, and smashed her with it.

† They knew each other from what fine journalists call "the prestigious Ross School in East Hampton," where the children of both men were enrolled. Yes, Ludwick had two kids with his estranged wife.

sen's house. The impact threw Hansen
halfway out of the car. Ludwick hauled him
the rest of the way out, dumped him on the
ground, and drove off. The car gave up after
a quarter mile. When the police arrived Ludwick was standing next to his expensive
German wreck, glassy-eyed, reeking of alcohol, swaying from side to side, nearly falling
down.* They found Hansen's wallet in the
woods where Ludwick had tossed it,
presumably — who knows? — so that he,
drunk Ludwick, wouldn't be associated with the body lying at
the far end of the oil trail the leaking Porsche had left. Yes,
"body." Hansen was dead.

Ludwick was charged with thirteen counts, including DWI,
felony aggravated vehicular homicide, and "leaving the scene of
an incident without reporting that it involves death," good for
a bounce inside of up to thirty-two years. At his hearing Ludwick insulted and infuriated Hansen's grieving relatives by taking out a two-inch-thick roll of bills and conspicuously
counting them while waiting for his turn before the judge. He
was released on $1 million bond.

Ludwick's freedom didn't last long. In January 2016, deemed
to be a flight risk, he was arrested and tossed into Suffolk
County Jail. Why? Funny story. He'd been in Puerto Rico taking sailing lessons and asking his instructor a lot of suspicious
questions.† The instructor told a fellow instructor, who happened to be an off-duty FBI agent, who did some research on

---

* The first question the police asked was whether there had been anyone in the car
with him. Ludwick's no-doubt-slurred answer: "Don't worry about him."

† Example: he wanted know how big a boat he'd need to cross to Venezuela.

Ludwick, was suitably appalled, and contacted a friend at the Southampton Police Department. The authorities soon descended upon Ludwick, who, they found, had transferred nearly $400,000 to a Puerto Rican bank account and was lining up a deal to buy an ocean-capable fifty-footer. Equally damning was their discovery of the vast, *Mad Magazine*-esque collection of Google searches his powerful Ivy-caliber brain had generated, including:

- "5 countries with no extradition"
- "Does Venezuela extradite to the US?"
- "Seeking citizenship in Venezuela"
- "What is expatriate life like in Venezuela?"
- "10 secrets to being a good liar"
- "Can I leave on a cruise with an arrest warrant?"
- "Percentage of bail jumpers caught"
- "How do fugitives escape?"
- "Why do fugitives get caught?"

The prisoner's attorney argued that his client was simply researching vacation activities for himself and his children. The Google searches? "Just a fantasy." No one bought it. Ludwick, bail revoked, remains in his Hamptons penal dormitory, awaiting trial.

Which leads us to the obvious question: Who is the most malignant real estate developer ever to come out of Penn, Sean Ludwick or **Donald Trump**? It's a tough one.

# Daniel Mason

*BA, Dartmouth College*

Meet Daniel Mason. He's no dummy, but he did some really stupid things. First, the no-dummy part: he graduated from Dartmouth in 1993 with a history degree and was accepted the following year at the Boston University School of Medicine. From which he never graduated. And that brings us to the stupid part.

On second thought, a little backstory might be helpful. Mason was born in Worcester, Massachusetts. When he was seven, his divorced mother moved with him to Israel. He grew up there and served in what he described as a special commando unit of the Israeli military where, he claimed, he was trained to be an assassin. When his military service was over he moved back to the US to attend Dartmouth.

Mason had a temper on him. At Dartmouth he was once arrested after some kind of eruption at a gym, but other than some psychological testing, nothing came of it. Oh, and he was arrested again the year he graduated, for threatening to kill his girlfriend after kicking his way into her house. Again, no prison time.

Okay, enough backstory. Now the stupid part...but, come to think of it, the stupid part overlaps with those anger explosions. We next see him as a medical student. A medical student with a pathological case of road rage. A twenty-eight-year-old Russian immigrant named Eugene Yazgur had the bad fortune to park his van in such a way that it blocked the forward progress of Mason's car. Yazgur said he'd move the van in a few minutes, but that wasn't fast enough for Mason, who thought he'd speed things along by slashing Yazgur's face, quite badly, with a blade.

Mason was found guilty of assault, and because he appeared to be a nice, normal, white med student, was given probation rather than jail time. But this is America, so Yazgur sued for damages. He won, and on March 1, 2001, Mason was ordered to pay him $118,000 over the next twenty years. "You'll never see a penny," Mason reportedly hissed at Yazgur in the courtroom, which you'd think would be cause for a bailiff or a prosecutor or the judge to step forward and—admittedly, this is speculative; we're not lawyers—fucking *tase* his ass, or something.

But no. Here's what did happen. At 1:30 the next morning Daniel Mason repeated the "he'll never see a penny of it" trope to his roommate, J. D. Smith, adding, informatively, "I'll kill him first." Later, appropriately wearing a black hat, Mason drove over to where Yazgur lived with his Great Dane, Samson, and a roommate, twenty-five-year-old Michael Lenz. Somehow—we assume it was easy for a former commando—he slipped into their apartment. Of course he had a gun or two. First he shot Lenz several times, killing him. Then he found Yazgur's bedroom and shot him in the face. Apparently Mason wasn't such a great assassin, though. Yazgur, not dead, tried to flee. Mason kept shooting, hitting him in the chest and both legs before he felt his work was done. On the way out he shot and killed Yazgur's dog. He then drove to Boston Medical Center to start his rotation at 7:00 a.m.

Yazgur, shot as many as eight times, was a mess after seventeen surgeries, but he survived. Despite his difficulty talking—a bullet had mangled his tongue and destroyed several teeth—he testified for two days at Mason's trial.

Daniel Mason, Dartmouth '93, was sentenced to life without parole for the first-degree murder of Michael Lenz, plus a second life sentence for home invasion, plus a concurrent nineteen-to-twenty-year sentence for the attempted murder of Eugene Yazgur.

Alas, prison's gain was medicine's loss: when he committed his crimes, Mason was two months away from receiving his medical degree from BU.

# Cotton Mather

*BA, Harvard University* ★ *MA, Harvard University*

In 1639, three years after the founding of Harvard College, Increase Mather was born in the Massachusetts Bay Colony. Seventeen years later he graduated from Harvard, became a minister (like his father and three of his brothers before him), married the daughter of a minister, and quickly became one of the most influential voices in the religious and political life of the colony. By age fifty-three he was president of Harvard.

His son, Cotton,* born in 1663, was only fifteen when he graduated from Harvard. (Which is impressive. Or is it? Back then, people died at a much younger age. Which means—and, yes, the idea is horrifying—teenagers were adults! Adjusted for the average life expectancy of the time, fifteen then was like twenty-five now.) Anyway. At age twenty-two, Cotton Mather took over from his father as pastor of Boston's North Church. In the Mather tradition, young Cotton was soon a force to be reckoned with in matters spiritual, secular, and, later on, scientific (he conducted pioneering experiments in plant hybridization). Great!

Then came the not-so great: before he was thirty, he had succeeded in orchestrating the series of legal debacles, religious embarrassments, and scientific *shandas*† that endeared him (in

---

* Don't ask. They were *Puritans*. We wonder whether he had a sister named Cottonelle.

† The word *shanda* is Yiddish for a disgracefully shameful thing. It's root, root, root for the home team; if they don't win, it's a shame. If they lose to the by-far-worst team in the league, it's a *shanda*.

a bad way) to history, not to mention to playwright Arthur Miller: the Salem witch trials. And the thing is, the whole Satanic-possession hoo-ha might have been nothing more than a twisted manifestation of Cotton's daddy issues, i.e., the need to prove that he, too, was a Big Man in Boston. After all, which of us hasn't thought, "Father continues to disdain my Accomplishments. For this Reason I must needs assert mine own Virtues and Abilities, the better to Shew him I am Worthy"?*

It so happens that Increase Mather was on record as being lukewarm toward the whole witch business. Not that he didn't believe in witches. Of course he believed in them. He just wasn't sure what to do about them. Cotton, perhaps seeing this as a way to differentiate himself from old dad — to create his own "brand," as we now say — saw the opening, and went for it.

Cotton Mather's main contribution to the witch controversy was to argue in favor of "spectral evidence." The term referred to complaints presented by people (usually children) that they'd been tormented by "emanations" of someone accused of being a witch. Which is to say, not by anything the "witch" had actually said or done, but rather, stuff she...you know...*emanated.*

Now, we have a name for that phenomenon, too. When we detect that another person is emanating at us, we accuse him or her of "having attitude," or "showing 'tude" or, more spectrally and Salem-y, "throwing shade." All these kinds of emotional harm have at least one thing in common: the harmer has to be in the same physical place as the harmee.

Not so with spectral evidence! The "specter" (i.e., the witch's spirit) could do things without the presence of the witch her-

---

* Cotton Mather didn't actually say or write this. This is us, "doing" him. Not bad, huh?

self. "Witnesses"—generally the very people who were the witch's accusers—would testify, for instance, that "Cottonelle [to choose a name at random] scratched at mine eyes, pinched mine forearms, and verily kissed mine lips, then choked me."* This sort of testimony was used as evidence that the accused, though far, far away at the time, was guilty of assault causing bodily harm, or whatever the charge mayeth have been.

Don't that beat all? Say you don't like someone. You start thinking about her. That becomes a fantasy about her attacking you. You call the police to complain about her emanations assailing you and tormenting you and hitting you upside the head. The police take your word for it, because "spectral," and there's no way to prove it didn't happen. And so they arrest her. She's tried and, because nobody wants to be seen defending the devil (who could be anywhere and influencing or impersonating anybody), she's found guilty and sentenced to death by hanging in the town square. It happened. Twelve people before 1692, and then twenty-four people at Salem, were tried as witches, found guilty, and executed.

Many opposed this, even at the time, so one can imagine the vigor with which Mather advocated the prosecution and punishment of these poor women (and a few men). Eventually, the locals had misgivings about the spectral-evidence business. A judge and twelve jurors of the Salem trials issued formal apologies for their roles in the convictions. Nevertheless, although sanity eventually asserted itself and spectral evidence was deemed inadmissible, Mather defended his advocacy of it in a book entitled *Wonders of the Invisible World*, published in 1693. A merchant named Robert Calef was so outraged, and so worried that Mather would try to revive the witch trials, that he wrote a

---

* Us again.

book critical of the trials, mockingly entitled *More Wonders of the Invisible World,* in 1700. When Increase Mather read the book, it so enraged him — how darest anyone mock mine spawn! — that he burned it in Harvard Yard. Yes, the president of Harvard, burning a book.

Meanwhile, Cotton Mather continued on his overachieving trajectory, writing more than four hundred books and pamphlets, preaching, helping steer the growing colony, and — get this — roping in a wealthy London-based businessman by the name of **Elihu Yale** to contribute to a college start-up in New Haven, Connecticut. And perennially agitating to have himself, Cotton Mather, appointed president of Harvard, just like dad.

It never happened. Alas.

# Lyle Menendez

*Princeton University Dropout*

You might argue that it's wrong to include in this book someone who was suspended from Princeton during his first semester, never to return. We'd argue right back that in this case the
magnitude of the monstrousness compensates for the minimal
Ivy exposure. If we were feeling really argumentative, we'd
assert that, just maybe, even a fraction of a semester at Princeton can irreparably warp an impressionable young mind. In
any event, Lyle Menendez, Princeton dropout, made our cut.

Lyle and his younger brother, Erik, were the sons of Jose and
Kitty Menendez. Jose, a hard-driving first-generation American, had emigrated from Cuba as a child, earned an accounting
degree from Queens College,* worked his ass off, zigzagged
upward through the ranks of various industries, and finally
earned a slot not far from the pinnacle of American capitalism
as a highly compensated show-biz executive in sunny
California.

But Jose's success did not extend to his and Kitty's child-
rearing. Possibly in rebellion against Jose's high expectations,
possibly because they knew their parents would bail them out
of whatever trouble they got into, possibly because they were
twisted, greedy little pricks, Lyle and Erik launched a plan to
break into their neighbors' houses in Calabasas and steal
expensive stuff. They managed to pull off two burglaries, net-

---

* Pardon us. We should have said "lowly, non–Ivy League Queens College."

ting more than $100,000 in cash and jewelry, before a friend turned them in.

Jose's response was to make them return the loot while reprimanding them for getting caught.* And, in order to protect Lyle's chances of getting into Princeton — one of Jose's big American dreams — he convinced the authorities that Erik, just eighteen, had masterminded the crimes. This neatly got Lyle off the hook and kept Erik from being saddled with an adult criminal record. Dad then quickly moved the family to a biggish house in Beverly Hills,  just far enough away from Calabasas that none of their new neighbors were likely to have heard of Lyle's and Erik's burgle-tastic past.

Lyle did indeed get into Princeton. We'll report only two items about his tenure there. First, he drove an Alfa Romeo, courtesy of his parents, which he told a classmate was, and we quote, a "piece of shit" compared to the Porsche he deserved. Second, he was caught cheating on an exam and was slapped with a one-year suspension. So Jose wouldn't have to explain to anyone why his Ivy League son was back in Beverly Hills so soon, he insisted that Lyle stay in (if not *at*) Princeton through the academic year.

When Lyle did return home, he and Erik hatched a plan, based largely on the plot of the film *Billionaire Boys Club* (and the real-life Ponzi-cum-murder scheme it was based on),† to

---

* To us, that's called "schizophrenogenic parenting." The message — "You did a bad thing! And you should have known how to get away with it!" — is, shall we say, *mixed*.

† And on a screenplay Erik and a friend cowrote that had a plot almost identical to the one Erik and Lyle hatched for real. It would have been a nice piece of evidence, practically a preconfession, had it been allowed at trial. Which, tragically, it wasn't.

murder their parents and claim their inheritances ahead of schedule. Their plan was simple, involving nothing but easily obtainable guns and ammo. On August 20, 1989, Jose and Kitty stayed home while Lyle and Erik pretended to be out with friends. At around 10 p.m. the boys slipped into the den, where their father was watching television with their mother dozing by his side. The first shot, a point-blank blast to the back of dad's head, woke mom. She flew off the couch but before she could escape they shot her in the leg and sent her sprawling to the floor. As she scrambled, they fired several more times, shredding her body and pulverizing her face. Blood and guts everywhere. Then, in a stylish cinematic flourish, they kneecap-shot each parent in order to plant the thought "Mob hit!"* in the minds of crime-scene investigators. The lads then hopped into a car, dumped the guns, and tried to establish an alibi by seeing a movie and afterward hanging with friends. Then they returned home, "discovered" their slaughtered parents, dialed 911, and played the part of a couple of nice rich kids who were deeply upset, practically unhinged, by the grisly scene.

Soon enough the boys dried their tears and got busy consoling themselves with their $14 million windfall. Lyle bought himself that Porsche 911, plus a Rolex, plus a restaurant he favored back in Princeton; Erik hired a full-time tennis coach to help him compete in professional tournaments overseas. Together, and without even bothering to offload the family murder-manse, they bought a pair of penthouse apartments in Marina del Rey, trotted the globe, explored luxury dining, and pursued countless other richy-rich activities.

Six months after the double parricide, the brothers' spending bender was cut short by their arrests. The first trials ended

---

* It was a thought that did not "take."

deadlocked after their mutual lawyer thoroughly flummoxed the juries with megatonnage of tabloid kibble featuring tales of the sexual abuse poor Lyle and Erik had suffered at the hands of their allegedly psychopathic parents. The second pair of trials reached more satisfying conclusions: life in prison without parole for both murderers.

So here's what you'll do the next time an obnoxious friend or relative proudly informs you that he or she, or his or her kid, got into Princeton. You will pause thoughtfully for a moment, sigh sadly, and say, "Didn't one of those little twerps who killed their parents get in there?"

# J. Ezra Merkin*

*BA, Columbia University ★ JD, Harvard University*

Poor Ezra Merkin. All he did was help people invest their money with Bernie Madoff.

Okay, that's not exactly accurate. See, he had his own hedge funds, including one called Ascot Partners, and because people liked him and thought he was a stand-up guy—especially fellow congregants of the Fifth Avenue Synagogue—they were happy to invest with him. But it wasn't just about familiarity, friendship, *mishpacha*. Ascot appeared to be solid; the *Wall Street Journal* said Merkin was "revered for his ability to ferret out value in…bombed-out stocks and distressed bonds," and was hands-on, adopting "a selective approach in evaluating potential investment situations, generally concentrating on relatively fewer transactions that he can follow more closely."

It didn't hurt that he was conspicuously successful, with an $11 million eighteen-room apartment in the best building on Park Avenue, $300+ million worth of Mark Rothkos, and mountains of other impressive shit. He could hold forth on many subjects. He had such gravitas. His nicknames were Ezra the Wise and The Rabbi, for Christ's sake. Moreover, he was the son of the founder of the Fifth Avenue Synagogue, probably the wealthiest *shul* in the world. And J. Ezra was its president! What could possibly go wrong?

---

* Those seeking pubic-wig jokes in this entry will be severely disappointed.

In reality, Ascot was not a hedge fund, but a chute leading directly to another hedge fund, and that other hedge fund was not a hedge fund either, but Madoff's Ponzi swindle. Merkin's clients gave him their money with the understanding that he would tend it responsibly and profitably. Instead, he reamed off his management fee* and secretly slipped the dough to Madoff—who wasn't even a member of his blue-chip temple! If and when Merkin was asked whether Ascot had anything to do with Madoff, he lied and said that supersafe Morgan Stanley, not sketchy Madoff, was safeguarding the swag.

All in all, Merkin funneled around $2.4 billion to Madoff from 1992 through 2008, earning himself fees (some deferred) of close to $500 million. He may have been a useless money manager, but he was a hell of a salesman.

Who were the suckers? We'll start with Yeshiva University. Merkin, a prominent board member and chairman of its investment committee, directed about $15 million of the school's endowment to Ascot,† for which he received his customary fee. Conflict of interest? Priceless!

Yeshiva was one of more than thirty nonprofits Merkin helped become even less profitable. New York Law School gave him $3 million. New York University: $24 million.‡ SAR Academy, an Orthodox Jewish school: $1.3 million. The foundation of real estate mogul and New York *Daily News* owner Mort

---

* Which supposedly pays for the expertise of those running the fund. In this case, that expertise consisted of knowing the location of Bernie Madoff's money drop.

† Perhaps not so oddly (in this particular small world), at a certain point Bernie Madoff became treasurer of Yeshiva University. Could he have chosen to steer money directly to his fund without allowing Merkin to dip his wick? Perhaps, but we imagine he was too kind, too generous, for that.

‡ According to NYU's attorneys, Merkin had ignored warnings from his associate Victor Teicher that Madoff was a scammer. For the record, Teicher was in federal prison for insider trading while he worked with Merkin.

Zuckerman: around $30 million. The Harlem Children's Zone: $2.7 million. Bard College (Merkin was on the board): $3 million. Elie Wiesel's Foundation for Humanity: $37 million — nearly its entire endowment.

And of course there were plenty of non-nonprofit clients. Something called the Calibre Fund: $10 million. Dr. Noel Wiederhorn: at least $1.75 million. Ira Rennert, owner of the biggest, ugliest house in the nation and chairman of the board of the Fifth Avenue Synagogue:* $200 million!

We know all this because the Madoff implosion and the gory details of investors' losses — such as the Ascot money vanishing down Bernie's reeking sinkhole — was a huge news story. In 2009 New York State charged Ezra the Wise with civil fraud for "steering $2.4 billion in client money into Bernard Madoff's Ponzi fraud without their permission" while claiming he was the active manager of said money. He had to resign as manager of his own hedge funds, which were placed in receivership, and agree to pay $410 million to settle the New York attorney general's lawsuit, of which $405 million was to go back to his former clients,† $5 million to the state.

Unsurprisingly, Merkin claimed he was shocked — shocked! — to learn that Madoff was a crook,‡ despite knowing that quite a few finance experts were suspicious of Madoff, and despite Merkin's once joking, semiwittily, that "Charles Ponzi would lose out because it would be called the 'Madoff scheme'" one day. Merkin also claimed to have lost a pile of his own

---

* The total hit to synagogue congregants was around $2 billion, leading to the tabloid coinage "Temple of Doom."

† Whose net gain on their investments, therefore, worked out to minus 83 percent.

‡ Thereby exposing himself as either a terrible money man (since he didn't clock that Madoff's absurdly consistent high returns were impossible); or a liar; or delusional.

money to Madoff, which supports his argument that he didn't know he was dealing with a criminal while undermining any argument he may ever make that he is not a boob.

All in all, a sorry episode and, as they say, bad for the Jews. And not so great for Columbia and Harvard, either.

# Judith Miller

*BA, Barnard College\* ★ MPA, Princeton University*

We have badged Judith Miller a "Disgrace to [Her] Profession," but that's only correct if her profession is defined as "journalist." If, however, you choose to define her profession as "right-wing flack," then she's doing a heck of a job.

The young Miller, already known for her raging career hunger and turbocharged story pursuit, was hired by the Washington bureau of the august *New York Times* in the late 1970s to help the Gray Lady compete with the *Washington Post*, then fresh from its Watergate triumph. Over the decades Miller proved to be a hardworking reporter, covering a number of beats (often returning to the Middle East and terrorism), cultivating many sources, and giving her bosses what they wanted. That included a Pulitzer, shared with colleagues, for a January 2001 series on al-Qaeda. Her reporting put her in contact with many of the neocon types who infested the **George W. Bush** administration. This came in handy after September 11, 2001: Miller had great access to the schemers who, even before bin Laden struck the United States, were planning to invade Iraq. Saddam had nothing to do with 9/11, of course, but the attack gave the Bushies nearly all the cover they needed.

---

\* We hear your stern-but-fair objection: it's not exactly an Ivy. But it is one of the Seven Sisters, it is and always has been extremely cozy with Columbia, it is across the street from Columbia, many Columbia classes are open to Barnard students and vice versa, at graduation Barnard grads receive diplomas that say "Columbia University" on them, and in any case she also has a master's in public affairs from the **Woodrow Wilson** School at Princeton, so please shut up already.

And, almost single-handedly, Judy Miller gave them the rest. In the run-up to the Iraq war, the *Times* front page was home to many a Miller scoop about Saddam's weapons of mass destruction. Her info, much of which turned out to be false, often came directly from the neocons or their pet Iraqi, Ahmed Chalabi; her stories were among the most powerful weapons of mass deception in the administration's propaganda arsenal. Many Americans were convinced that somehow getting rid of Saddam would...well, who knows what it was supposed to accomplish. But 9/11! Plus oil! Whatever. The crowning moment of the Miller-neocon operation went like this:

1. Vice President DICK CHENEY's chief of staff, Scooter Libby (Yale BA, Columbia JD), slips Miller and *Times* reporter Michael Gordon the factoid that a shipment of aluminum tubes was seized on its way to Iraq. The tubes are supposedly used in the enrichment of nuclear materials; Saddam needs them for the nuclear weapons he's absolutely definitely building.
2. On Sunday, September 8, 2002, the tale is presented in the form of a Miller-Gordon scoop on the front page of the *Times* with the headline "U.S. Says Hussein Intensifies Quest for A-Bomb Parts."
3. Now the genius part. On the same day the story appears, top members of the administration — CHENEY, DONALD RUMSFELD, Colin Powell, Condoleezza Rice — fan out to the Sunday talk shows and *cite the story to justify the invasion of Iraq.*

As the *New York Review of Books* said, the tubes became "a key prop in the administration's case for war, and the *Times* played a critical part in legitimizing it." Six months later: the Iraq invasion. Mission accomplished, Judy!*

That war, as you surely know, was a moronic, pointless, and utterly misbegotten disaster from which the world may never recover. As we said, most of Chalabi's and the neocons' "intelligence" about Saddam's WMDs was false. Ergo, since these were Miller's prime sources, most of her reporting was inaccurate. One salient example: The aluminum tubes were not for building nukes.

Because Miller was a scoop machine and had highly placed, albeit dishonest, sources, the *Times* was reluctant to reassign her to the mass transit beat, or business, or obituaries. But in May 2004, shortly after the Bush administration tossed Chalabi overboard, the paper went so far as to admit that some of its reporting had relied too heavily on him and other liars. It refrained from dissing any of its reporters, but finally, in October 2005, the *Times* public editor all but admitted that a lot of Miller's work had been "inaccurate." Shortly afterward, she exited the paper.† Since then she's practically made a career of arguing, counterfactually, that history has proved she was right and her critics wrong.‡ Who employs her now? One guess. Go on. Try. You'll never g— Oh. Yeah. Right. Fox News.

A final note. In November 2015, after ISIS terrorists killed 130 innocent people in Paris, Miller took to Twitter. She didn't apologize for her role in creating the conditions that led to the

---

* Same "mission" as with **Bush**. Same "accomplished," too.

† We're ignoring the eighty-five days she spent in jail protecting a source—Scooter Libby again—in the Valerie Plame affair. So sue us.

‡ She once explained that her job "isn't to assess the government's information and be an independent intelligence analyst myself. My job is to tell readers…what the government thought about Iraq's arsenal." In other words, to be a stenographer for powerful prevaricators. Which is pretty much what her critics say about her.

attack; that's not her way. Instead, she wrote: "Now maybe the whining adolescents at our universities can concentrate on something other than their need for 'safe spaces'..."

We wonder what the students of Barnard and Princeton have to say about this esteemed alumna who, upon learning of the massacre, criticized *them*.

# Charles Murray

*BA, Harvard University*

DPr E R RWN

Charles Murray is the pet sociologist of the regressive-conservative right. He says, and probably believes, that he is "a social scientist, and a damned good one." But one look at who sponsors his work and his objective scientist *bona fides* start to seem ultra-iffy.

Murray's book *Losing Ground,* published in 1984, focuses on what it claims is the futility of social benefits programs such as welfare and affirmative action, and calls for their abolition. He wrote the book while a fellow at the Manhattan Institute, a right-wing think tank whose mission is to "develop and disseminate new ideas that foster greater economic choice and individual responsibility." Yeah—*that* old right-wing wheeze. The institute's board features, among others, national empath/loon Peggy Noonan and **William Kristol;** it advertises praise from DICK CHENEY and Rudolph "Noun Verb 9/11" Giuliani. With such sponsorship, is it any wonder that pretty much the only people to hail the book's conclusions are the conservatives who agreed with it before it was ever written? For everyone else, the book features misleading statistics, goalpost-moving changes of definitions, and conveniently ignored contexts, all in the service of promoting the elimination of welfare.

But never mind that. Murray became a star with *The Bell Curve* (1994), which he wrote with the late Richard Herrnstein (of Harvard). It purports to prove that the IQs of African Americans are genetically—fatedly—lower than those of whites. (But don't get cocky, white people. Your IQs are lower than those of Asians.) To prove its by-definition racist (and implicitly eugenicist) thesis, *The Bell Curve* cherry-picks IQ tests, manipulates statistics, and proffers research of highly dubious provenance. Why? Why else — to make the case for abolishing government laws, subsidies, and ameliorations regarding black people.

As for its sponsorship and credentials, oh brother. If you thought the Manhattan Institute cast a pall of prejudice over Murray's first book, getta loada *Mankind Quarterly*. Born in Edinburgh in 1960, this publication is an anthropological journal founded and funded by what we might call "genetic white supremacists." Its founder, Robert Gayre, advocated apartheid in South Africa, defended "racialism" from its unfortunate association with the Nazis, and once testified in a trial that, in his opinion, blacks were "worthless." *Mankind Quarterly* gets its money from the Pioneer Fund,* which — despite its denial of any connection to white supremacism or, um, Nazis — retains its charter-enshrined mission: "race betterment, with special reference to the people of the United States."

One of Murray's and Herrnstein's key advisors on *The Bell Curve* was Richard Lynn, a psychology professor at the University of Ulster in Northern Ireland — an associate editor of *Mankind Quarterly* who has received $325K from the Pioneer Fund.† Lynn has, in his writing, agreed with the view that "the poor and the ill" are "weak specimens whose proliferation needs to be discouraged in the interests of the improvement of the genetic quality of the group, and ultimately of group survival." A *Newsday* article cited him as saying, "What is called for here is not genocide, the killing off of the population of incompetent

* Founded by WICKLIFFE DRAPER and at one point run by **Harry H. Laughlin**.
† The Pioneer Fund was also rather fond of **Arthur Jensen**.

cultures. But we do need to think realistically in terms of the 'phasing out' of such peoples.... Evolutionary progress means the extinction of the less competent. To think otherwise is mere sentimentality."

"Race betterment." Improving "the genetic quality of the group." "Incompetent cultures." Yes, and "phasing out" peoples via "the extinction of the less competent." With intellectual guidance like that, who needs Nazis? Murray denies that his book is a eugenics tract and insists that his focus is not black people, but social class. But considering the fact that one key chapter harps on "dysgenesis" (the genetic deterioration of a population), that denial seems disingenuous at best. A social class is not a genetic phenomenon. But a race — at least to the Murrays of the world — is.

The upshot of all this is that government shouldn't waste money on trying to improve educational (or any other) opportunities for the poor unfortunates whose genetic inferiority, of course, is not really their fault. What *should* the genetically blessed do instead? Set a good example. That, in fact, is the theme of Murray's book *Coming Apart* (2012), which ascribes the "decline" in American society to the abandonment by the rich white upper class of its traditional obligation to instruct the lower orders by showing them how to behave.

Yes, really.

Murray has won for himself a life of wealth, luxury, and esteem by lending "scientific" support to policies beloved of racists, crackpots, and anti-Semites — and, more important, of conservatives. Because after all: If a government's efforts to aid its citizens are doomed to fail, why bother? Which means, why pay — why even levy — taxes?

Who *does* this? One answer: a small-town boy acting out.

Murray grew up in tiny, idyllic Newton, Iowa. His father was stern, his mother insufferable. He enjoyed "taking pride in per-versity" at Harvard by wearing his ties with the fat end short. After college, in 1965, Murray joined the Peace Corps. He went to Thailand, where he lived in a village that he came to regard as a model society. "Essentially, most of what you read in my books I learned in Thai villages," he told Bill Kristol in 2014. "I suddenly was struck first by the enormous discrepancy between what Bangkok thought was important to the villagers and what the villagers wanted out of government. And the second thing I got out of it was that when the government change agent showed up, the village went to hell in terms of its internal governance."

There's the right's favorite sociologist: a nerd who defies The Man by wearing his tie wrong, and who longed for the America of 2014 to be more like a Southeast Asian village in 1965.

# Ralph Nader

*BA, Princeton University ★ LLB, Harvard University*

Hunched inside a rumpled suit, Ralph Nader may not look like a man driven by ambition. But do not be fooled. He holds himself in the same imperious self-regard as any other Ivy League monster. Not that he hasn't done his bit to help humanity, with the non-profits he's spawned, the corporate nimrods he's skewered, the seat belts he's caused to be buckled, the shoddily made cars he's caused to be unshoddily unmade.

And yet, when we think of him, we can't help recollecting that terrible election of 2000, when the forces of purest E-vil (the Republican Party, the Supreme Court, etc.) conspired to hand **George W. Bush** a huge prize he had not won, after which…well, some other stuff happened.

That year, Nader ran as the Green Party presidential candidate, against both Republican Bush and Democrat **Al Gore**. While Nader had zero chance of winning, polling indicated that he would likely do much better than he'd done in the 1996 election, when he received all of 0.71 percent of the votes. As the race tightened, knowledgeable observers began to speak of Nader as a potential spoiler. In the closing weeks of the campaign, many wondered whether he would (from the point of view of the center-left and left) do the right thing and, if there was a chance he might suck just enough votes from Gore in certain states to tip the race to Bush, withdraw.

It all came down to Florida, where Nader campaigned heavily, accusing the major parties of being identical, calling Gore and Bush Tweedledee and Tweedledum, and making it clear that those who were nervous that his candidacy might lead to a Bush presidency could go fuck themselves. (That wasn't his language, but somehow one knew what he meant.)

In the end, more than 5.8 million votes were cast in Florida. According to the official-if-disputed count, Bush beat Gore by a mere 537 votes. Close! Except that nearly 100,000 people voted for Nader. Sure, they wouldn't all have voted for Gore had Nader dropped out. Some wouldn't have voted at all. And, yes, some would have voted for Bush.

It's even likely that some registered *Democrats* would have switched from Nader to Bush. (Gore was a terrible campaigner: "Lockbox! Lockbox! Lockbox!") According to some widely respected and unbiased political observers, it's not out of the question that Bush would have won by a *wider* margin had Nader dropped out. Granted, such a voter's thought process would have to have been something like: "Hmm. I was going to vote for the Green Party's antiestablishment, anti-big business, left-of-the-Democrats candidate. But if he's not running, I guess I'll vote for a bumbling rich kid who couldn't make a living in oil *in Texas*, and whose millionaire Republican father has been head of the CIA, vice president, and president." Then again, some exit polls suggested that there were people who actually did think this way, so go understand people.

Or don't bother. Instead, ask yourself, "Did Nader's 100,000 votes make it possible, or at least easier, for the GOP vote-miscounting squad and the Supreme Court to foist Bush on the nation?" Even if the answer is "Maybe; we just don't know," there are some things we definitely do know. We know that Nader was well aware that the race was exceptionally tight, that his candidacy might throw it to Bush, and that he insisted it didn't matter because Bush and Gore were essentially the same person, the Democrats and the GOP the same party. But he was wrong about that. It did (and does) matter. Nader's the-parties-are-identical position was no different from today's media's self-serving/lazy/cowardly explanation for gridlock in Washington, the "both sides do it" false equivalence that passes as insider savvy or "balance" while being demonstrably untrue. Nader had a chance to wield a political superpower, to bow out, endorse (and maybe campaign for) Gore, and with that one act, help—or at least try to—defeat the titanically mediocre Bush. Instead, from the lofty height of his idealism, ego, and political purity, he colluded in ushering in eight years of bumbling monstrosity.

Like any smug ideologue who's been drinking his own Kool-Aid for too long, Nader cannot admit when he's wrong. He was and is unapologetic about his role in helping elect George W. Bush. He's happy to list all the reasons why his vanity run for president couldn't possibly have had anything to do with the Florida debacle. And it's a good bet he's still insisting that there's no difference between Democrats and Republicans, and therefore that the events of 9/11 and the ensuing clusterfuck in the Middle East would have gone no differently under a Gore presidency. And if he does think that, he must be the only person in the country who does.

So, sure, Ralph Nader did some good work. Tragically, he seems incapable of understanding Voltaire's famous dictum *Le mieux est l'ennemi du bien* (The best is the enemy of the good). Which, in the context of Ralph Nader, means that certain egomaniacs turn a blind eye when their precious principles, so noble in the abstract, wreak disaster when they intersect with the real world.

# Walter M. Noel, Jr.

*MA, Harvard University ★ LLB, Harvard University*

If you are reading this book in the normal, tried-and-true manner—starting at the beginning and working your way toward the end—you already know about **J. Ezra Merkin.**\* So we'll make it easy for you. Think of Walter Noel and Ezra Merkin as the same person.

The End.

Sigh. Okay. Like Merkin, Walter Noel is a former alleged money manager,† but transposed to the key of WASP (as in Greenwich, Connecticut, although he was spawned in Alabama). Noel's firm, the Fairfield Greenwich Group, like Merkin's Ascot Partners, pretended to know what it was doing—superior knowledge of the marketplace, due diligence, a principal who wore nice clothes and was a good salesman, blibbity blah blah— but in fact, like Merkin's organization, was simply cramming its customers' money down the Bernie Madoff Asset Incinerator®. With your kind indulgence, we will now switch metaphors to state that Fairfield Greenwich was in fact the largest-diameter sewer pipe flushing money to the Cesspool of Madoff®, more than $7 billion vs. Ascot's puny $2.4 billion.

There are more stories to be written about Noel—about his

---

\* If you started at the end and are reading backward, or are reading the entries in random order, or have an attention-deficit issue and find yourself reading a paragraph from here, a sentence from there, a footnote from someplace else, then it doesn't matter what we say *here* since none of it is making sense to you anyway.

† Also with a law degree from Harvard, plus a Harvard MA in economics.

wealthy Brazilian wife; their beautiful house in Greenwich; their beautiful apartment in Manhattan; their five beautiful, highly accomplished, multilingual, Ivy-educated (well, three out of five) daughters with five rich, handsome, internationally bred spouses; the way Walter had to pay back only a fraction of what he took from his clients, which is why he was able to maintain the lifestyle of a Wall Street genius even after he was revealed to be a simpleton and a cheat—but face it, we couldn't stand to write those stories, and you couldn't stand to read them.

So: The End.

Okay, we will do one more thing for you. We'll reveal the headline of the current, up-to-the-minute-as-of-this-writing Fairfield Greenwich Group website:

**Welcome to the Fairfield Greenwich Securities Litigation Class Action Settlement Website***

---

* At the bottom of the first page there is a note stating that the website is not operated by any of the people who pissed away the money, but by a claims administration firm whose job it is to help the unfortunates who fell for Noel's sales pitch get their money back.

# Dr. Mehmet Cengiz Öz

*BA, Harvard University* ★ *MD, University of Pennsylvania*
★ *MBA, University of Pennsylvania (Wharton)*
★ *Columbia University Faculty*

He's a distinguished cardiothoracic surgeon—a heart transplant specialist at New York Presbyterian/Columbia University Medical Center! He's also a popular TV personality! Who touts dubious remedies! Dispenses New Age-y pseudoscientific advice! Spouts  uninformed anti-GMO propaganda! Promotes paranormal beliefs! And hosts crackpots who say things like: Cancer is a fungus that can be cured with baking soda! He's Mehmet Cengiz Öz—TV's handsome Doctor Oz!

You'd think it would be enough for anyone to be a professor, vice chairman of surgery, and working surgeon at a major hospital, not to mention an inventor and holder of lifesaving medical patents. But that wasn't enough for Dr. Oz. He wanted more. He wanted fame—big-time, *TV-level* fame. And he understood that you don't get that kind of big, fat fame by being a do-your-job academic and a just-the-biomedical-facts-ma'am kind of doctor.

Nope, fabricating and stockpiling mass quantities of fame requires being known and loved by mass quantities of the masses. And to attain that, you've got to promote crazy shit. Not just a little bit, either. Lots and lots of crazy shit. And so it came to pass that Dr. Oz, with a big assist from Oprah Winfrey, got himself a TV show, or maybe several TV shows, some radio shows, and a bunch of book deals — who can keep track? — and, voilà, big-time fame!

What he seems not to have realized, despite his obvious smarts, is that publicly promoting tons of crazy shit doesn't go over so well with other members of the medical profession — or anyone else who is enthusiastic about healthcare, the scientific method, or objective reality. *The British Medical Journal* analyzed Oz's recommendations and found that over half of them had no scientific basis. "Oz," said *The New Yorker*, "has been criticized by scientists for relying on flimsy or incomplete data, distorting the results, and wielding his vast influence in ways that threaten the health of anyone who watches the show."

Ponder that for a second: a TV doctor, over half of whose recommendations are iffy at best and downright dangerous at worst. With medical advice like that, who needs disease to feel sick? And that was mild compared to the denunciation leveled by a group of prominent American physicians in a letter to the Columbia College of Physicians and Surgeons (yet another Ivy League institution, incidentally). It included lines such as "Dr. Oz has repeatedly shown disdain for science and for evidence-based medicine" and "he has manifested an egregious lack of integrity by promoting quack treatments and cures in the interest of personal financial gain." (The manufacturers of certain "miracle" products touted on his shows have also sponsored those shows. You expect this sort of thing in infomercials about self-washing frying pans or vegetable juicers that pick you up at the airport. Not on shows about health, hosted by actual doctors.)

For his support of faith healing and communication with the dead, among other procedures not taught at the University of Pennsylvania School of Medicine, the James Randi Educational Foundation — whose agenda is to expose parapsychological, paranormal, or psychic fraud — has awarded him its Pigasus Award an unprecedented three times.

Mehmet Oz was a highly respected doctor who, with admirable focus and superhuman determination, transformed himself into a media superstar. But he's become so much more than that. Indeed, his achievement has exceeded the fantasies of the most driven double- or triple-Ivy-League-degree holder. He is a self-invented institution.

He is America's Quack.

# James Perkins
*Harvard University Benefactor*

Harvard's Perkins Professorship of Astronomy and Mathematics was established in 1842 with an endowment from the estate of James Perkins, Jr., a highly respected businessman whose many commercial activities included investments in real estate, a theater, an iron foundry, bridges, toll roads, textile mills, hotels, railroads, canals, and coal mines. But before all that, Perkins and other members of his family were involved in the shipping industry. As in the import-export business. The goods they were importing-exporting, that launched them into high finance and big-time philanthropy, were slaves and opium.

Perkins was born in 1761 into a family of prosperous Boston merchants, and he grew up in the heady atmosphere of the American Revolution. As young adults, he and his younger brother Thomas were friends with George Washington—yes, *the* George Washington—as well as the Marquis de Lafayette and many of the other revolutionary figures whose names you'd recognize in a second. By his early twenties James was sailing back and forth between Santo Domingo—now called Haiti—and various American ports. Pleasure cruises? Not for the slaves belowdecks. This was the leg of the triangle trade* in which some of the humans originally abducted in Africa and now "working" in Santo Domingo† were imported to America, along with various products of the sunny

---

* Details? See the **Brown Family**.

† In 1782, there were 300,000 to 500,000 slaves on the island.

Caribbean. James Perkins, soon joined by brother Thomas, supplemented the slave trade* with horses, dried fish, and flour.

The Perkins brothers were nothing if not opportunists. By 1788 they had their own fleet and were importing slaves directly from Africa to American ports. China had opened for trade in 1785; shortly thereafter the brothers put together a complex network dedicated to buying furs from the Pacific Northwest and selling them profitably in Asia.

And, sure, selling otter skins to the heathen Chinese was cool. But soon the Perkins men discovered something even cooler: Opium! In 1804 they built a ship specifically for smuggling Turkish opium into China and named it the *Mandarin*, in honor of the Chinese officials they were bribing to allow their illicit business to flourish. Demand was so great—to masses of Chinese people, opium was the opiate of the masses—that in 1815 they opened a Mediterranean office to support their Turkish operation. The money kept rolling in.

James Perkins died of pneumonia in 1822. A local newspaper eulogized that there was "not a shadow of suspicion of anything derogatory" to be cast upon this model citizen, and Josiah Quincy III, Speaker of the Massachusetts House of Representatives, future mayor of Boston, and sixteenth president of Harvard University, wrote that he "was formed on the noblest and purest model of professional uprightness; without guile, without reproach."

He left $20,000† to endow a chair at Harvard. When his wife died in 1842, the funds were delivered.

---

* For the record, their father, like many Boston go-getters, had also been involved in the triangle slave trade.

† In today's dollars: $67 trillion, we guesstimate.

# Richard Perle

*MA, Princeton University*

During the Carter administration, Richard Perle began his adventures in government as a senior staff member for Henry "Scoop" ("The Senator from Boeing") Jackson on the Senate Armed Services Committee. When Reagan took office, Perle enthusiastically helped him promote physicist/madman Edward Teller's idea for a "missile shield," the Strategic Defense Initiative (SDI). Amusingly — sort of — this scheme involved shooting down Russian ICBMs using *fricking laser beams*, both land-based and *on platforms in outer fucking space*. In the end, scientists announced that the technology for SDI was at least ten years away,* and the project was sent to the backest of burners. It was during Reagan's administration that Perle acquired the nickname "The Prince of Darkness." He didn't like it, but it stuck.

Then the Soviet Union dissolved, the Cold War ended, and Perle looked around for some other cause. He found it in the Project for the New American Century (PNAC), a neoconservative think tank cofounded in 1997 by Ivy League Monster Extraordinaire **William Kristol**. PNAC's mission was to urge more aggressive use of US military force around the world — specifically in Iraq.

When **George W. Bush** was selected president and 9/11 happened, everybody's dreams — of "preemptive" military attack,

---

* It's *always* at least ten years away.

of deposing Saddam Hussein and "liberating" Iraq, of swaggering around on the world stage as the brain trust guiding the United States to global domination—came true. As early as 1990, Perle had been working with Iraqi businessman (and secret Iranian operative) Ahmed Chalabi to remove Saddam. Once the Twin Towers came down, Perle, **Douglas Feith,** and the gang established not one but two secret offices in the Pentagon to find, buff up, if necessary invent, and channel intelligence about Iraq to support arguments in favor of invasion. Perle insisted, on media large and small, that Saddam "had ties" to the terrorists, which he didn't, since most of them were from Saudi Arabia.

In this, Perle and the other neocons acted in service of a worldview dominated, as one writer put it, by "warrior worship, existential conflict, and extreme moral righteousness." Sounds thrilling, yes, especially if the warriors being worshipped aren't you or your children. In an interview he gave shortly before the invasion of Iraq, Perle invoked the term he had used during Reagan's presidency: "total war."

> No stages....This is total war....If we just let our vision of the world go forth, and we embrace it entirely and we don't try to piece together clever diplomacy, but just wage a total war...our children will sing great songs about us years from now.

It's worth noting, now and forever, that with W's installation—especially after 9/11—the neocons got *everything they wanted:* a malleable president, a powerful and conscience-free vice president, a complaisant Congress, a fully mobilized military, an unlimited budget, a credulous press, and enough public support to fulfill their wettest of dreams.

The war began. The Iraqis were shocked and awed. Then, after the military walkover, the occupation began and Americans at home were awed and shocked at the mendacity underlying the war's rationale and the conquerors' inept management of the aftermath. Within a few years, Perle expressed regret at having supported the invasion but denied responsibility for having promoted it. "Huge mistakes were made," he said, employing the famous passive voice. "And I want to be very clear on this: They were not made by neoconservatives, who had almost no voice* in what happened."

Well. It's true that the implementation of the invasion and the conduct of the occupation were the domains of W, RUMMY, and the State Department. But it was Perle, along with the other neocons, who blamed 9/11 on Saddam Hussein; who predicted a quick and easy victory; who denied any real Shiite–Sunni tensions; who insisted we'd be greeted as liberators. No voice in what happened? Surely you're too modest, Mr. Perle. (May we call you Dick?)

Of course, promoting America's global dominance is good clean fun, but it's also necessary to, as George W. Bush once said, "put food on your family." In this regard — the methodology behind the putting of food on his family — Perle's record is spotty, if not fully checkered. He was criticized for recommending that the army buy gear from an Israeli company that a year earlier had paid him $50,000. In 2003, while chairman of the Defense Policy Board Advisory Committee, Perle was accused by the journalist Seymour Hersh of having improper business dealings with Saudi investors. In March 2004, Perle took money from a company to promote its sale of assets to a Hong Kong–based firm in spite of the FBI's and Pentagon's opposition. He

---

* Except, perhaps, a passive one.

194

was accused of having breached his fiduciary responsibilities as a director of another company; the SEC called for him to return his compensation. He demanded payments for interviews. Finally, *Politico* reported in 2011 that Perle traveled twice to Libya with the Monitor Group, a consulting firm of which he was a senior advisor, as part of an effort to "burnish Libya's and [Muamar] Qadhafi's image" in the United States.

Still, what's a little influence peddling and hypocrisy among friends? Perle's legacy will be the Iraq war he promoted with half-truths and dire warnings. Ten years after the launch of the war, when NPR reporter Renee Montagne asked Perle whether it had been worth it, he replied: "I've got to say I think that is not a reasonable question. What we did at the time was done with the belief that it was necessary to protect this nation. You can't a decade later go back and say we shouldn't have done that."

This is contemptibly self-serving and, frankly, monstrous — and certainly something for our children to sing great songs about years from now.

# Ezra Pound

*MA, University of Pennsylvania*

Can you be a great poet and still be a monster? Can you be a monster and still be a great poet? Is it possible to be a great poet, or even a good one, if you're as much concerned with spreading your (fringe, nutty) ideas about economics — which lead you into the vilest kind of prejudice — as you are with poetry?

Behold the legacy of Ezra Pound: modernist pioneer, friend and confidant and editor and encourager of many of the early twentieth century's great writers, innovator of poetic forms, admirer of Mussolini, fan of Hitler, and monstrous anti-Semite. "Controversial" doesn't begin to describe him, both during his life and after his death.

The good news: He helped discover and mold the work of Ernest Hemingway, James Joyce, Robert Frost, and T. S. Eliot. He got Eliot's *The Love Song of J. Alfred Prufrock* published and arranged for the serialization of Joyce's *A Portrait of the Artist as a Young Man*. He invented a poetic style everyone called imagism and he called imagisme. He contributed two snappy one-liners to the phrase book about modernism: "Literature is news that stays news" and "Make it new." He wrote many good poems, maybe one great one (*Hugh Selwyn Mauberley*), and a vast, uncompleted masterwork that exasperated everyone and which he despaired of at the end of his life (*The Cantos*).

The bad news: Like many, Pound was deeply disillusioned by World War I. He began to think about the war's causes and ended up with a diagnosis of capitalism and usury. That led to anti-Semitism. He moved to Italy in 1924 and nine years later met with Mussolini. Pound tried to share with Il Duce his views on economics; the man who invented the word "fascist" brushed them aside, but later Pound said that he had "never met anyone who seemed to GET my ideas so quickly as the boss."

Starting in 1939 Pound contributed anti-Semitic articles to Italian newspapers. During the war, the Italian government paid him to make hundreds of anti-Semitic radio broadcasts equating Franklin D. Roosevelt with "the Jews" and calling for America to stay out of the conflict. From a broadcast on March 14, 1942: "You let in the Jew and the Jew rotted your empire, and you yourselves out jewed the Jew.... And the big Jew has rotted EVERY nation he has wormed into." He also wrote for publications owned by Oswald Mosley, the British fascist, calling the Third Reich "the natural civilizer of Russia." On the day Germany surrendered, Pound told an American reporter that Hitler was "a Jeanne d'Arc, a saint."

The broadcasts were of course monitored by the United States, and in 1943 Pound was indicted in absentia for treason. He was arrested and placed in an outdoor cage in isolation for three weeks. He was transferred to the States, charged with treason, and admitted to St. Elizabeths Hospital in southeastern Washington, DC, for the next twelve years, starting out in a ward for screaming maniacs but soon moved to a more congenial wing. It was there that he concentrated on *The Pisan Cantos*, which he had begun in that outdoor cell.

Although he repudiated his anti-Jewish stance in public

(perhaps to bolster the case for his release), he kept to it in private, refusing to talk to psychiatrists with Jewish-sounding names, denigrating people he disliked as "Jews," and championing the known forgery *Protocols of the Elders of Zion* (which had come out in 1903). Among his friends were anti-Semites and a famous Klan member. Bear in mind that, however unaware of the concentration camps the world was in 1946, the public was plenty aware — as was Pound — by 1949, when *The Pisan Cantos* won the Bollingen Prize, administered by the Library of Congress. The furor was immense.

In 1958 Pound's friends hired a lawyer who moved to dismiss the wartime indictment, and it worked. Pound was released. He went back to Italy, but visited England and the States, where he was both feted and deplored. He became increasingly depressed. He thought *The Cantos* were "a mess" and told an interviewer, "I spoil everything I touch.... I have always blundered." He died just after turning eighty-seven, in 1972.

Toward the end Pound told Allen Ginsberg, "Any good I've done has been spoiled by bad intentions — the preoccupation with irrelevant and stupid things." Then, knowing full well that Ginsberg was Jewish, he added, "But the worst mistake I made was that stupid, suburban prejudice of anti-Semitism." "Stupid" because wrong, immoral, bigoted, ignorant, and a belief used to justify mass slaughter? Or because "suburban"?

Does it matter?

# Raj Rajaratnam
*MBA, University of Pennsylvania (Wharton)*

One of the reasons to choose a superelite college, it is said, is for the contacts: "It's not what you know, it's who you know." Is it possible that there's another side to that platinum-plated gold coin of a platitude? Raj Rajaratnam might think so.

He was born in 1957 to a well-off Sri Lankan family. His father was a successful businessman, the head of Singer Sewing Machine in South Asia. When he was a teenager, Rajaratnam's family moved to England to escape the political turmoil in Sri Lanka. There he went to college, earning an engineering degree before heading off to Philadelphia to pursue an MBA at Wharton.

Like any good MBA, he was smart, ambitious, and in love with money, or wealth, or perhaps affluence. Or maybe he just had a crush on riches beyond measure. And, like many a freshly minted MBA, he obtained employment with the noble banking industry. He rose quickly through the ranks and by the age of thirty-four was president of some boutique banky thing, then started a hedgey thing at the banky thing. He spun off the hedgey thing, and behold: *the Galleon Fund!*

By 2008, just before the economy had an aneurism, Galleon was valued at $7 billion. In 2009, although Rajaratnam was personally worth $1.8 billion,* the fund was down to a scant $3.7 billion. And by the end of 2009, Galleon had sailed into

---

* Which is more than anyone born in Sri Lanka had ever been worth.

the sunset, right off the edge of the earth, closed for business, sayonara. How can that be?

It can be because in October 2009, Rajaratnam was arrested for using insider-trading tips to illicitly rake in more than $60 million; his investors, naturally, jumped like rats off a sinking ship—rats who demanded their money back. In 2011, Rajaratnam was found guilty and sentenced to eleven years of prison time, the longest ever for insider trading; he also had to pay civil and criminal penalties amounting to more than $150 million.

Of the insiders who had whispered sweet corporate secrets in his ear, two had been his classmates at Wharton. Might he have been better off, and less likely to have ended up a white-collar jailbird, had he gone to a not-quite-so-eminent institution?

We wonder what Raj thinks.

# William Z. Ripley

*MA, Columbia University ★ PhD, Columbia University*
*★ Harvard University Faculty*

Adolf Hitler did not need the imprimatur of a respected Ivy League professor to convince a large swath of the German populace that he, and they, were blessed to be members of the master race. The question is: Who inspired Hitler to think there even *was* such a thing as a master race? Answer: A respected Ivy League professor! Or two! Sure, Germany had a history of self-lovin' braggadocio. But let's face it: when you're looking to push an agenda of racialist hate and nativist resentment, it never hurts to have a seal of approval from authoritative foreign (and, therefore, "objective") sources, who come equipped with prestigious academic credentials.

Herr Hitler? Meet William Zebina Ripley.

In 1890 Ripley earned his bachelor's degree in engineering at MIT, followed by a master's (1892) and a doctorate (1893) from Columbia. This was back in the day when you could knock off a PhD in less time than it takes Twenty-First-Century Man to make sense of the latest iTunes update — probably because a) there was so much less to know in ye olden days, and b) iTunes alone is more complicated in 2016 than the entire world corpus of engineering knowledge was in 1893.

After receiving his PhD, Ripley taught sociology at Columbia, then moved on to teach economics at MIT and then at Harvard, where he remained for the rest of his academic life. Indeed, despite having started as an undergrad in engineering, despite his advanced degrees in sociology, Ripley went on to become a noted economist, helping Teddy Roosevelt sort things out between the railroads and Big Coal, settling strikes, rationalizing the nation's rail system, advocating for corporate transparency, and much more.

But before his rebirth as an economist, in 1899, while still at Columbia, Ripley wrote a book—as one does—to pay for his children's college education. It was *The Races of Europe,* and it proposed race as the lens through which human history should be viewed. It put forward a classification system that divided Europeans into three racial groups, Teutonic, Mediterranean, and Alpine, based on geography and—in a made-up term that must have formed a single word forty yards long in German— "cephalic index," a.k.a. skull shape and size.

It was nonsense, of course, and not just by today's standards. There were sociologists, anthropologists, biologists, and non-ignorant civilians of Ripley's day who correctly insisted that there *is* no scientific definition of "race," no way to delineate where one alleged race ends and another begins, and no reason to impute inherent mental, moral, or physical characteristics to these imaginary entities. Nonetheless, Ripley's ideas were picked up by others in the nascent discipline of scientific racism. Among the picker-uppers was another Ivy man, **Madison Grant,** who in *his* book, which elaborated upon Ripley's, substituted "Nordic" for "Teutonic," declared it the best of all possible races, tossed in a pinch of eugenics, and—once "Nordic" was swapped out for "Aryan"—it was *"Auf wiedersehen,* science," and *"Guten Tag,* Adolf!"

Ripley moved on from bullshit racial theories to legitimate economic ones, for which he was widely praised when he exited this vale of tears in the early 1940s. Did his eulogizers praise *The Races of Europe*? Oh, who cares. What's important is that the book was a hit in its day. It surely, as intended, helped put his kids through school — as, indirectly, it helped put millions of other people's kids in death camps.

# Raphael Robb

*University of Pennsylvania Professor*

Raphael Robb got his BA at the Hebrew University of Jerusalem in Israel and immigrated to the United States in 1970. In 1981 he got his PhD in economics from UCLA. Three years later he joined the faculty of the University of Pennsylvania. Five years after that, he married Ellen Gregory. In 2004 Robb was granted tenure.

He was known for his contributions to evolutionary game theory—which, as we know you know, refers to the application of game theory to evolving populations of biological life-forms. In classical game theory, rational actors (i.e., human beings) make rational decisions within a context of rules and desirable goals (i.e., games). Applying a version of these principles (minus the "rational actors" part) to evolution answered a lot of questions, such as why individuals in animal populations would demonstrate "altruism," when everyone knew—supposedly— that evolution required each individual to maximize the probability of his or her own survival.

But following rules to attain certain goals can sometimes be harder than it looks, and while it's one thing to theorize about rational behavior, it can be another to adhere to it. On December 22, 2006, Robb and his wife argued—about their impending divorce and about the disposition of their house in King of Prussia, Pennsylvania. Then, as she was wrapping Christmas presents, Robb bludgeoned her to death—either with a chin-up bar or a crowbar, depending on whom you believe. In any case, the police mistook the gruesomeness of her injuries for the results of a shotgun blast.

Robb claimed the murder was the result of a burglary,* but nonetheless was arrested in January 2007 and pleaded guilty to a charge of voluntary manslaughter that November. The prosecutor was Bruce L. Castor, Jr., who commented, not entirely gracefully, "Professor Robb may be smarter than us, but he still is an amateur killer, and we are professional catchers of killers."

Robb was sentenced a year later, to five to ten years. He was granted parole in January 2013, but the ruling triggered a national uproar. After the testimony of the Gregory family and others, the board reversed its decision. The following year, the couple's daughter filed suit against her father for his appreciable assets. She won a judgment of $124.4 million, which economists refer to as "a fuck-ton" of money.†

All of this leads one to wonder: if *Ivy League faculty* members don't know better than to fly into an insane rage and murder their spouses, how can they expect students to behave any better?

---

* How original.

† Based on nothing but the stories of professors Raphael Robb and **Lawrence Scott Ward,** a stranger to our planet might conclude that all Ivy League economics professors are rich and evil.

# Michael Bruce Ross

*BS, Cornell University*

Many column inches of the May 27, 1981, issue of the *Cornell Daily Sun* were filled with the names of the students who would be graduating that coming Sunday. Among those listed under the heading "Bachelor of Science (Agriculture and Life Sciences)" was one Michael Bruce Ross. Another headline in the same issue read "D.A. Says Cornell Gorge Death Might Not Be a Suicide." It's the sad story of Vietnamese immigrant and Vassar graduate Dzung Ngoc Tu, a first-year Cornell graduate student in agricultural economics, whose body was discovered on May 17 in an Ithaca creek five days after her landlady reported her missing.

Suicide is always the first theory when someone ends up at the bottom of a gorge in Ithaca. But those who knew Tu described her as happy and dedicated to her work; they had no reason to think she'd been contemplating a gorge dive. Nor could anyone imagine that she'd had any enemies, or a boyfriend gone bad. Since her battered body had been immersed in churning water for nearly a week, Tu's autopsy was inconclusive: no discernible signs of foul play.

It remained an unsolved mystery for six years. That's when a man on death row in a Connecticut prison — he'd been arrested and convicted for the rape and murder of a teenager and subsequently confessed that he'd killed five other Connecticut women — belatedly admitted that he had also raped and murdered two women in New York State, starting with the first victim of his deadly spree: Dzung Ngoc Tu.

The convict was Michael Bruce Ross, serial killer and 1981 Cornell Agriculture and Life Sciences graduate. He killed Tu nineteen days before his graduation ceremony. His own execution-by-lethal-injection ceremony took place in 2005.

That — and the observation that a Life Sciences graduate was so dedicated to death — are all we can stand to say about him.*

* Other than that before Cornell, he'd graduated from the too-on-the-nose-named Killingly High School in Killingly, Connecticut.

# Isaac Royall, Jr.

*Harvard Law School Benefactor*

At the age of twenty-three, in 1700, Isaac Royall, Sr., looking to cash in on the best business opportunity of his time, moved from New England to the Caribbean island of Antigua, heart of the diabolical and lucrative triangle trade. Soon he was the owner of a plantation staffed by African slaves, the part owner of a slave ship, and the proprietor of a prosperous import-export enterprise that involved the movement not only of slaves but of sugar and rum as well. (For more on the triangle trade, see the **Brown Family** entry.) Royall had a good quarter century to fill his coffers in Antigua before God returned to His desk at last and unleashed the drought of 1725, the devastating hurricanes of 1733, the earthquakes of 1735, and the smallpox epidemic and slave revolt of 1736. At some point Royall decided that the grass was looking greener back in the colonies. By 1732 he had started to assemble a large chunk of real estate in Massachusetts to serve as the Royall family seat.

Isaac Royall, Jr., born in Antigua in 1719, moved with his family in 1737 to Ten Hills Farm, the magnificent new Royall estate. Accompanying them were at least twenty-seven slaves — more slaves than any other family in Massachusetts owned. When his father died just two years later, Isaac Junior, age twenty, inherited the 500-acre estate, the plantation in Antigua, and eighteen of the slaves. Not content to be an indolent heir, he became an active and successful real estate investor —

and a buyer and seller of slaves—known far and wide as one of the wealthiest men in the colony. He wasn't shy about displaying his wealth: he spent lavishly on imported furniture and china, supported the work of master silversmith Paul Revere, and rode around in a stagecoach staffed by liveried servants. By 1754 he was down to twelve slaves, which was still six times the slave count of any other family in the region. Along with his wealth came recognition: he was honored as a selectman in Medford, a justice of the peace, a member of the Governor's Council, and an Overseer of Harvard College.

Royall didn't fare so well when the American Revolution came. Although he was close to many who were leading the cause of separation from the crown, he was known for his conservative, loyalist leanings. This put him in enough danger that in April 1775, three days before the Battle of Lexington, which marked the start of the war, he packed up, freed his slaves, and left in a hurry for Nova Scotia. Considered an enemy of the new country, he was officially banned from returning. Nonetheless, in his will he left a bequest to Harvard for the establishment of a law professorship.

He died not long afterward, in 1781. It took a while for his gift to reach Harvard, as the estate had been confiscated by Massachusetts after Royall fled. In the end, all was forgiven and the heirs got their estate back. Honoring Isaac Junior's wishes, they donated a large sum to underwrite the first Harvard law professorship. Within a couple of years the professorship became the Law Department, which, as you've already surmised, grew up to become the Harvard Law School.

In 1936, 300 years after Harvard's founding and 155 years after Royall's death, the Harvard Corporation bestowed a custom-designed heraldic shield upon each academic unit. The

Law School's was an adaptation of Royall's family coat of arms, an azure field surmounted* by three sheaves of wheat. As far as we know, there were no protests back then, but the students and faculty of the early twenty-first century were mightily discomfited by that shield. To them, it might as well have been an azure field surmounted by three hanging trees with nooses rampant. They protested; they were victorious; the Royall-inspired shield was "retired."

At the time of this writing, Harvard Law School is, somehow, operating without a shield.

---

* Heraldry talk! Let's say.

# Antonin Scalia

*JD, Harvard University*

The monstrousness of Antonin Scalia cannot be overstated. He was a racist. A homophobe. A religious fanatic. A bully. And a smug little prick. So are many other people. The difference is that this prick had a lifetime appointment to the Supreme Court of the United States of America. When an ordinary prick behaves prickishly, you do your best to escape. But there's no escaping a Supreme Court justice: Scalia deliberately inflicted pain on millions of captive Americans. Herewith, a few examples of his pricky handiwork.

### Scalia and Race

Scalia wrote the dissenting opinion in a case brought by a white woman contending that she was refused admission to the University of Texas because — any guesses? That's right! Because she was white! And an affirmative-action black kid took her place!

Scalia insinuated that black students shouldn't be aiming so high: "There are those who contend that it does not benefit African-Americans to get them into the University of Texas where they do not do well, as opposed to having them go to a less-advanced school, a slower-track school where they do well.…Most of the Black scientists in this country don't come from schools like the University of Texas. They come from lesser schools where they do not feel that they're being pushed ahead in classes that are too fast for them.... I don't think it stands to reason that it's a good thing for the University of Texas to admit as many Blacks as possible."

Less advanced. Slower. Lesser institutions.

Do note that, starting in the late 1960s, Scalia taught law, first at the University of Virginia, then at the University of Chicago. Black students at both elite* institutions complained that he graded on a biased curve: if you were black, your grades curved downward. He seemed to delight in putting an F on a black student's work, and rarely did he deign to go higher than a C. His white students thought him a fair grader.

## Scalia and Homosexuality

"Many Americans," wrote Scalia in his dissent to a decision that tossed out a Texas law criminalizing gay sex, "do not want persons who openly engage in homosexual conduct as partners in their business, as scoutmasters for their children, as teachers in their children's schools, or as boarders in their home." Imprisoning homosexuals, his logic goes, will be applauded by these "many Americans" because "They view this as protecting themselves and their families from a lifestyle that they believe to be immoral and destructive." Those poor, poor Americans. Lock up the perverts! And while you're at it, try substituting "Jewish religious practices" or "Islamic lifestyle behaviors" for "homosexual conduct" in the above dissent. Why should a Christian have to endure anyone else's immoral lifestyle?

---

* Perhaps not as elite as Scalia's law school, but elite nonetheless. Only high-achieving students, regardless of color, were admitted.

In another dissent—this from a Colorado law banning discrimination against gays*—he said, disingenuously, that "it is our moral heritage that one should not hate any human being or class of human beings," then goes on to excrete some nice, steaming hate: "But I had thought that one could consider certain conduct reprehensible—murder, for example, or polygamy, or cruelty to animals—and could exhibit even 'animus' toward such conduct. Surely that is the only sort of 'animus' at issue here: moral disapproval of homosexual conduct." It's an animus Scalia shared, encouraged, and wallowed in, so, hey, let's criminalize the homos.

In the aforementioned Texas case, the attorney opposing the law making gay sex illegal cleverly pointed out that if nonprocreative sex is bad—a loony stance of the antigay faction then, logically, it should be illegal for straight couples to have sex unless they make a baby. Scalia countered with this gem: "It doesn't say you can't have any sexual intimacy. It says you cannot have sexual intimacy with a person of the same sex." So: to avoid breaking the law, gay people should simply start having normal, unperverted sex with a person of the opposite gender. Which is not a crazy thing to think if it's, say, 1954 in Elmhurst, Queens, you're a spoiled only child—the son and grandson of Italian immigrants—attending a Jesuit high school, and you a) have not only never (knowingly) met any gay people but would probably have hurled insults at them if you had, and b) believed in the actual, personal existence of the devil.

Some sixty years later the man was on the Supreme Court, and *he still thought that way.*

---

* Perhaps we oversimplify. In fact he was voting against a case challenging a law that made antigay discrimination illegal. Got it?

## Scalia and Religion

Speaking at Colorado Christian University*: "I think the main fight is to dissuade Americans from what the secularists are trying to persuade them to be true: that the separation of church and state means that the government cannot favor religion over non-religion." Actually, a close reading, or even a sloppy reading, of the Establishment Clause of the Constitution reveals the exact opposite of this Scalia trope. If the government has no say over the establishment of religion, it has no say over whether an individual American has to give a flying fuck about religion at all.

## But Wait! There's More!

Much more! But, alas, to keep our Scalia musings from expanding to the size of the *Encyclopædia Britannica,* we must cut it short here. Suffice it to say that Antonin Scalia diapered up his festering hatreds in deliberately obscurantist constitutional mumbo-jumbo—his "originalist" shtick—to make his prejudices seem to emanate from a dispassionate Olympus of rational reasoning and profound philosophizing, with perhaps a slug of old-time religion.

   Would he have been viewed as anything but a twisted little bigot—or seated on the Supreme Court—if he'd gone to a "lesser" law school?†

---

* A backwater religious redoubt—his kind of place, despite his Ivy League pedigree.

† Such as the recently renamed, Koch-funded Antonin Scalia Law School at George Mason University. George Mason almost went with "Antonin Scalia School of Law" but decided that the acronym, "ASSoL," resonated uncomfortably with its eponym.

# Jeffrey Skilling

*MBA, Harvard University*

For those who missed it, Enron was...well, it's not so easy to say what Enron was, other than an epic scam. The company was based in Houston. It started out in the mid-1980s as a merger between two natural gas companies. It was soon known for being super...what's the word?...oh, right: *innovative*. So innovative that *Fortune* crowned it America's Most Innovative Company six times in a row. It claimed gross revenues of $111 billion in 2000. In late 2001 it declared bankruptcy. Turned out, Enron's impressive innovative spirit was mainly focused on the invention of creative — i.e., fraudulent — accounting schemes. And the chief architect of that fraud was a Harvard MBA* named Jeffrey Skilling.

Skilling came to Enron in the late '80s as a McKinsey consultant on the make. CEO Ken Lay spotted his talent and snapped him up to head Enron's finance division. By the late '90s, Skilling was president and CEO of all Enron, reporting only to Lay. In 1999 Skilling introduced an online natural gas–trading operation that, to us, appears to have been something like eBay for energy; it was quickly adopted by nearly every energy company in the country.

Skilling's illegal activities were legend, but they're either too technical for a book of this nature or we're not fucking smart

---

* If you're thinking of applying to Harvard Business School, take a tip from Jeff Skilling. When asked during his admissions interview if he was smart, he replied, and we quote: "I'm fucking smart." Brilliant!

enough to understand them. Instead of a detailed explanation of what he did, we'll go a little impressionistic here to give you a sense of the man.

- After California deregulated the energy market, Enron was responsible for dozens of "rolling blackouts" designed to extort higher prices from energy consumers. (Deregulation, in brief, meant that commodities traders like Enron, not government regulators, determined the price of electricity. California's deregulation had been driven by campaign contributions the company made to legislators involved in the process.) Here's a joke Skilling thought was amusing during that period: "What's the difference between California and the *Titanic*? When the *Titanic* went down, the lights were on." Heh heh.

- In 2001, PBS's *Frontline* investigated the blackouts. Reporter Lowell Bergman noted that Enron invented electricity trading, which, he said, was the cause of California's energy problems. Skilling laughed, then parried that it's exactly the same as trading wheat or steel (which it's not; electricity is a public utility), then capped his self-serving argument by ludicrously asserting: "We are on the side of the angels." (Bergman could have replied, "Satan was an angel," but didn't.)*

- Between the summer of 2000 and the summer of 2001 the price of electricity in California more than tripled. The increase had nothing to do with the cost of producing the power and everything to do with traders, especially Enron.

- Skilling took home $132 million during the same period.

---

* Trust us. We read the transcript.

- When, during a conference call, a financial analyst pointed out that Enron was the only financial institution that didn't show a balance sheet or cash-flow statement to explain the earnings it claimed, Skilling wittily replied, "Thank you very much. We appreciate that—asshole."

Skilling resigned in August 2001, "for personal reasons," and sold off close to $60 million of Enron stock. In December the company declared bankruptcy. What Skilling knew was that Enron's financial success was an illusion* and the whole house of cards was about to come crashing down. Luckily, Skilling sold his stock before it collapsed from around $90 to pennies a share. Oh, wait. Did we say "luckily"? We meant "insider tradingly."

In 2006 Skilling was convicted of thirty-five charges, including insider trading. He was sentenced to twenty-four years and four months of prison time and a $45 million fine; in a subsequent bargain, the sentence was reduced by ten years.

When Skilling leaves prison he will be a widely despised man—but, unlike those who made the mistake of investing their life savings in the most innovative company of the 1990s, he'll still be rich.

---

* We're hoping you're not going to make us explain what they did to create that illusion. Okay, here's one thing: they created "special purposes entities," companies Enron owned and used as fake trading partners to create fake profits. Can we move on now?

# Eliot Spitzer

*BA, Princeton University ★ JD, Harvard University*

Bernard Spitzer was a successful New York real estate developer. His son Eliot grew up in the cushy Bronx enclave of Riverdale, prepped at the elite Horace Mann School (itself the site of a monstrous faculty-on-student sex-abuse scandal), and did his undergrad work at Princeton. Next, buoyed by unwavering confidence, dazzling LSAT scores, and his family's wealth, young Eliot gained admission to Harvard Law, became an editor of the *Harvard Law Review,* and married another Harvard Law student, Silda Wall. The world was his oyster, success in politics his goal.

Eliot Spitzer's first act on the big stage was to join the Manhattan district attorney's office, where he made a name for himself as head of the labor racketeering unit — not, as you might think, a group charged with investigating corrupt obstetricians, but rather the guys concerned with busting mafiosi. His second act in politics was to run for, and win, the office of New York State attorney general (helped by a campaign "loan" of dubious legality from his father).

As AG, Spitzer took down white-collar criminals and made a big stink over the huge compensation package of the chairman of the New York Stock Exchange, earning the abiding hatred of many Big Swinging Dicks on Wall Street. He also

zealously targeted prostitution rings. Women's rights advocates asserted that since prostitutes were as much victims as
perps, the law needed to be changed to make it easier to go after
the johns. Spitzer agreed. As a result of his efforts, New York
soon adopted the toughest anti-sex-trade legislation in the
nation.

Boosted by his high profile as attorney general, Spitzer won
a landslide victory in the 2006 election for governor of New
York. Imagine the delight of many Wall Streeters, and the dismay of supporters who had lauded his sex-trade victories, when,
in March 2008, the *New York Times* published "Spitzer is Linked
to Prostitution Ring," revealing that the governor himself was
a john, "Client 9" at a $1,000-an-hour call girl enterprise clas-
sily named Emperors Club VIP. As the story unspooled, we
learned that during his time as attorney general and governor
Spitzer had spent as much as $80,000 on prostitutes. (Can you
imagine? Who has that kind of money? Who has that kind of
*time?*) And what a breath of fresh (read: stale) air on the left.
This was the sort of appalling/hilarious revelation of hypocrisy
and sin usually reserved for televangelists, right-wing
congressmen,* and Catholic priests.

Federal investigators stumbled upon Spitzer's nasty predilection while conducting what they thought was a money laun-
dering investigation: Spitzer had made a number of fishy-looking
bank transfers that the feds took as a sign of graft. Nope: the
governor was clean as a whistle, corruption-wise. Unfortunately, he was as dirty as sin, frequenting-prostitutes-wise, and
the public airing of his dark side pretty much canceled out the

---

* Yes, "men," since sex scandals in Congress almost always involve male congressper-
sons. Which is not to say that we're not open to hearing about illicit behavior among
congresswomen, because we totally are. And, of course, the other parties in those
scandals can be women, men, boys, girls, and whatever else is left.

belligerent white-knight persona he'd taken so much care to cultivate. (After all, this is the United States. We're descended from Puritans. What sophisticated people—like the French—might call "ironic behavior," we call "hypocrisy." Yes, we're saying outright that the United States isn't France, *and never will be!*)

Within two days of the *Times* article's appearance, Spitzer—his loyal wife silently suffering by his side—resigned as governor. Silda Wall Spitzer, a model for Julianna Margulies's character in *The Good Wife,* waited five long years to resign from the marriage.

# Kenneth Starr

*MA, Brown University*

**D** **RWN**

With a BA from George Washington University, an MA from Brown, and a JD from Duke, son-of-a-minister Ken Starr had a lot of schooling. After obtaining the law degree Starr did his share of lawyering, but from the start he had his eye on the public sector. He landed there in 1983, when Ronald Reagan appointed him a judge on the US Court of Appeals, District of Columbia Circuit. Then, in 1989, the first President Bush appointed Starr US solicitor general. After returning to private practice at a fancy DC law firm, Starr was hired by the Senate Ethics Committee in 1993 to examine the diaries of GOP senator Bob Packwood, who had been accused of sexual abuse by a boatload of women and foolishly took detailed notes* on his depredations. Starr's notes on those notes led the committee to recommend that Packwood be ejected from the Senate; he resigned before he could be fired.†

In 1994, Starr, still in private practice, was tapped to work part time as independent counsel on the investigation of the Arkansas real estate deal known as Whitewater—which was *big*, since it involved, among many others, **President Bill** and First Lady Hillary Clinton. Although Starr was seen by both

---

* More than 8,000 pages of them. Between the abusing and the note taking, it's not clear how Packwood had time for anything else.

† He died in prison. Just kidding. He became a rich, successful lobbyist.

political parties as a moderate — too moderate for some of the more conservative Republicans — it appears that Whitewater unbalanced him. Maybe the desire to win eventually overcame the desire to be a decent human being: he morphed from milquetoast to attack dog.

Note that the Whitewater investigation was instigated and ginned up by a cabal of right-wing loonies funded by billionaire loon Richard Mellon Scaife. Although Starr wasn't a charter member of the cabal, he ended up as an avid lubricator of their wettest dreams. In the course of the investigation, Starr prepared a document for the House of Representatives alleging that Bill Clinton had perjured himself and maybe ought to be impeached. The idea of impeaching Clinton, presented not by a certified wackjob but by the stolid-seeming Starr, had the Republicans salivating uncontrollably.

Sadly for them, Whitewater was already winding down. Fifteen Arkansans were convicted of various fraud and bribery charges, including Jim Guy Tucker, the state's governor, who resigned. But no crimes were traced to the Clintons, and there were no grounds for impeachment. Before Starr could slink back to his high-paying law gig, however, something new came along: the death of Vince Foster, deputy White House counsel and former law colleague of Hillary Clinton. At which point Starr's Whitewater investigation jumped the rails, and voilà — to violently switch metaphors — was reborn as Starr's Vince Foster investigation. But despite the mouth-breathers' claims that Hillary had personally murdered Foster and then covered it up, or something like that, Starr and everyone else who actually investigated the matter pronounced the death to have been what normal people had all along known it to be: a suicide.

Then the retooled Vince Foster investigation magically became the investigation of Bill Clinton's sexual dalliances with one Paula Jones and—after Starr's personal request to the Department of Justice—Monica Lewinsky. Actually, all three (and more*) of these investigations overlapped; it's just easier to describe the implacable, kaleidoscopic madness of the Scaife gang's pursuit of the Clintons by laying them out sequentially.

This ferret-fuck continued until the release in 1998 of the material that became *The Starr Report,*† possibly the dullest sexually explicit book ever written. This led directly to a) the GOP getting their asses kicked in the November midterm elections, b) Speaker of the House Newt Gingrich resigning for overselling the Clinton scandals as a boon to GOP candidates, and c) Clinton's impeachment‡ in December. The work of the nation was essentially placed on hold for the nearly two months of the blow jobs proceedings, which ended with the president being acquitted of the blow jobs charges and the nation wondering what the hell all that had been about.

What did Starr accomplish with his mad pursuit of the Clintons? Mainly this: in polls taken after the 2000 presidential election, the top reason **George W. Bush** voters gave for their choice was the candidate's "moral character." Which of course was relative, i.e., to Bill Clinton, which is not what the average GOP voter would necessarily have thought if Clinton's morals hadn't been publicly hammered every day for the previous six years. While the catastrophe of the Iraq war could not have been predicted prior to the election, the awfulness of a George W. presidency was entirely predictable, and was indeed

---

* The firing of White House Travel Office personnel! Abuse or misuse or whatever of FBI files! Rose Law Firm high-jinx! Madison Guarantee monkeyshines!

† Available from Amazon.com for $0.01 (plus $3.99 shipping) as of this writing.

‡ For perjuring himself about blow jobs and obstructing justice concerning blow jobs.

predicted by many. Thanks, Kenneth Starr and the rest of the vast right-wing conspiracy.*

After the impeachment fiasco, Starr moved on to the things lawyers do after a high-profile government gig, viz. lucrative private practice and academic appointments. In 2010 Starr was named president of Baylor University, a Baptist institution in Waco, Texas. His initial project was to make sure the school remained a member of the Big 12 athletic conference. Alas, his concern for the well-being of the Baylor athletic program over-shadowed his concern for the well-being of the Baylor women who were being raped by Baylor athletes. Which, apparently, is why Starr turned the other cheek to reports of sexual violence on campus. And why, in May 2016, he was fired as president.

Yes, Ken Starr — prissy scold, tool of hypocrites, and servant of posturing moralizers — flames out for his inaction and excuse-mongering in an *actual* sex scandal. Ain't karma a bitch.

---

* The phrase Hillary Clinton first used in 1998 to characterize, accurately, the forces hounding her and her husband.

# Clarence Thomas

*JD, Yale University*

What is it about Supreme Court Justice Clarence Thomas we—
and so many—find so objectionable? Is it the silence he displays
on the bench, suggesting—since he has no questions—that he
always knows in advance how he's going to rule? His negligence
in failing to declare more than $600,000 of his wife's lobbying
income? His lifelong admiration of *The Fountainhead* and his
requiring that his staff watch the ludicrous, self-parodying
1949 movie version?

Or maybe it's just his horrible, often seemingly willfully
cruel, voting record.

**Antonin Scalia,** in his time, had a reputation as the court's
"fiery conservative," but in fact Clarence Thomas is, as it were,
more Catholic than the pope—to the right even of Scalia, and
one of the most conservative justices in US history. As such, he
has been involved in the following terrible decisions:

- *Bush v. Gore,* which destroyed, for at least a generation, the
  idea that the Supreme Court held itself above party politics
  and judged issues according to the disinterested legal lights
  of its members. (Or are we being too sensitive? After all, as
  Scalia explained, "Get over it.")
- *Connick v. Thompson,* in which Thomas, writing for the five-
  man majority, tossed out a verdict in favor of a defendant
  who was wrongly convicted of both an armed robbery and
  a murder, after the prosecution withheld *ten* exhibits of

exculpatory evidence. Thompson, the defendant, was sent to death row for eighteen years, until the official misconduct was discovered mere weeks before his scheduled execution. A jury awarded the man $14 million plus another million for attorneys' fees, and the Fifth Circuit Court of Appeals upheld it. The defendant was exculpated on both charges, but Clarence Thomas ruled against the compensation, holding that the DA (Harry Connick, Sr.*) couldn't be held responsible for a single errant prosecutor (even though five different prosecutors were involved in suppressing the evidence) mishandling a single piece of evidence (which was actually one of ten).

- *Shelby County v. Holder,* striking down the Voting Rights Act's requirement that racist states be required to obtain federal clearance for any changes to state voting laws. Thomas said such racially prejudicial conduct was no longer in evidence in such states as Mississippi and Alabama — which, as soon as the toner was dry on the ruling, instituted voter ID and other vote-suppressing laws. Thomas was thus a doctor telling a diabetic she can stop taking insulin shots, since they've worked so well up until now.

- *Citizens United v. FEC,* because Thomas believes all limits on federal campaign contributions are unconstitutional and should be struck down. In his view, the Founders clearly felt that insurance companies, securities and investment firms, real estate interests, and commercial banks are "persons," and should be able to pour unlimited money into our political process. Sure, it *looks* like the very definition of corruption. But it's really "speech."

---

* Yes, his father.

His dissents are a laugh riot, too. They include:

- *Foster v. Chatman,* in which Thomas disagreed with the other seven justices, who upheld an African American defendant's claim that African Americans had been specifically dismissed, via peremptory challenge, from his jury. (The defense found the prosecutors' notes, which included a list of potential jurors, with each black individual's name highlighted in green and with an identifying B beside it.) This was just the latest example of how Thomas has consistently ruled against programs designed to help African Americans and rejected findings of racial discrimination.
- *Obergefell v. Hodges,* which invalidated same-sex marriage restrictions. Thomas rummaged through the attic of Anglo-American legal history and cited John Locke, the Magna Carta, eighteenth-century British legal philosophy, natural law, and the Declaration of Independence — none of which are germane to a Supreme Court ruling. And shouldn't an "originalist," of all people, know that? It was in his *Obergefell* dissent that he contributed the extraordinary thought that

> …human dignity cannot be taken away by the government. Slaves did not lose their dignity (any more than they lost their humanity) because the government allowed them to be enslaved. Those held in internment camps did not lose their dignity because the government confined them. And those denied governmental benefits certainly do not lose their dignity because the government denies them those benefits. The government cannot bestow dignity, and it cannot take it away.

(This from a Supreme Court nominee who, accused of sexual harassment by Anita Hill, thundered righteously that he was being subjected to "a high-tech lynching" when in fact what he was undergoing was a job interview.)

- *Texas Department of Housing and Community Affairs v. The Inclusive Communities Project,* which upheld the use of disparate impact claims under the 1968 Fair Housing Act. Joined by **Samuel Alito** in his dissent, Thomas noted that racial imbalances sometimes appear without prejudicial intent, and cited the NBA as evidence. "Racial imbalances do not always disfavor minorities.... In our own country, for roughly a quarter-century now, over 70 percent of National Basketball Association players have been black. To presume that these and all other measurable disparities are products of racial discrimination is to ignore the complexities of human existence." No, given the context, it doesn't make sense.

- *Voisine v. United States,* in which the court upheld federal law prohibiting those people convicted of misdemeanor domestic assault from buying a gun. This dissent was a rare example of Thomas expressing sympathy for an individual versus a state. He objected to the majority opinion because "it imposes a lifetime ban on gun ownership for a single intentional nonconsensual touching of a family member." Appalling, yes — to Thomas, a citizen should be prohibited from owning a gun only *after* he uses it to shoot his wife. Still, we look forward to using the phrase "intentional nonconsensual touching" in a threatening manner next time we're drunk and feeling frisky.

There's more, but you get the idea. Clarence Thomas, who

once affixed a sticker reading "15 cents" to his Yale Law School diploma—Why? We'll tell you why! To inform it, and the world, just what he thought of its value, that's why!—rose from southern rural poverty to the apex of the American legal profession. In so doing, he has used the law, the Constitution, and "originalism" as a trio of clubs with which to beat the very idea of the individual, and to enact some sort of bizarre revenge against a society he feels has treated him badly. Which, to us, seems more than a little insane.

But don't take our word for it. Take, instead, the word of none other than Antonin Scalia, as quoted by Jeffrey Toobin in *The New Yorker*:

As for Thomas's place on the Court, it's difficult to improve on Scalia's analysis, which I heard him give at a synagogue a decade ago. Scalia was asked about how his judicial philosophy differed from Thomas's. "I'm an originalist," Scalia said, "but I'm not a nut."

# Donald J. Trump

*BS, University of Pennsylvania (Wharton)*

*I went to an Ivy League school. I'm very highly educated. I know words. I have the best words.*

— Donald J. Trump

From the moment he appeared on the public stage it was clear that Donald Trump was a Dickens character come to life: an exuberantly vulgar business ogre with an evocative, fake-seeming name who would do whatever it  took to get his way, or who would say whatever he could think of to at least *appear* to be getting his way. New Yorkers knew him as a loutish, pouty, media-crazed local real estate developer and failed casino operator. He had it all: a Zsa Zsa–esque hi-glam foreign-born blond wife* who was the first to refer to him as "The Donald"; his name plastered (okay, welded) onto every building he bought; and, in each square-jawed, man-of-affairs, uberserious photograph, an adolescent schoolboy's idea of a

---

* Who maybe, as Trump claimed, really *was* an alternate on the 1972 Czechoslovakian Winter Olympics ski team, but, in fact, really really wasn't.

commanding visage. So what if he was a widely derided buffoon among people of good, or any, taste? When you're a narcissist, there really *is* no such thing as bad publicity.

And when, in 2004, he ascended to a prime-time slot as host of NBC's *The Apprentice* and made "You're fired!" his signature line (which he tried, but failed, to copyright), who could possibly be shocked that it was a cross between a sadistic Japanese game show and *Idiocracy*? Trump had, through an amazing combination of tirelessness, ambition, and obnoxiousness, accomplished the impossible. He had become both an actual businessman and a comic-book cartoon of himself.

Nonetheless, despite Trump's decades of exposure, only the most diligent observers recognized the true malevolence lurking beneath the buffoonish behavior and otherworldly hair. Then, in 2011, he came out as a "birther," peddling the baseless smear that Barack Obama was not a Hawaiian-born Christian but a Kenyan-born Muslim. "He doesn't have a birth certificate," he told Fox News, adding incoherently: "He may have one, but there's something on that, maybe religion, maybe it says he is a Muslim."

Was it a surprise to learn that this self-branding loon, this "real estate mogul" whose businesses declared bankruptcy four times, this professionally bullying TV personality, this *superrich Ivy League graduate* was ostentatiously jumping into bed with the lowest, dumbest, creepiest, most bigoted faction of the American political right? Not to those who were onto him from the beginning. Back in the early 1970s, after young Donald's father anointed him president of the family business, the Justice Department sued the Trump Organization for violating the Fair Housing Act by refusing to rent to black people. Trump, employing what would become a signature move,* punched back by counter-

---

* Inspired by his mentor, **Roy Cohn**.

suing the government for a randomly large number of dollars—in this case 100 million of them. He also loudly protested that if dark people on welfare were allowed into his buildings, entire communities of nice white people would, *en masse,* rise up and leave the city. Needless to say, his lawsuit was tossed out of court and he was legally compelled to rent to qualified people of color. Any color. There were no reports of thousands of nice white people attempting to flee New York City.

Much more may be said about Donald J. Trump. But this is not that kind of book: we will leave his racist, jingoistic presidential campaign—not to mention his insistence that he won by a landslide despite garnering nearly three million fewer votes than Hillary Clinton, his prep school "military" record, his Vietnam draft deferments, his nutzoid claim to be "the most militaristic person you will ever meet," the thinness of his skin, his claims that "the blacks* love me," his marital escapades, his narcissism, his boorishness, his outer-borough concept of taste, the shoddiness of his edifices, his use of illegal-immigrant laborers, the truth about his net worth, his bromance with and role of useful idiot to Vladimir Putin, the book by Adolf Hitler he kept by his bedside, the fraudulence of Trump University, the Chinese origin of his ties, the failure of his line of hi-kwality steaks, his tweeting addiction, his grabbing of pussies, and countless other matters of public record—to the many chroniclers, biographers, psychologists, apologists, and humorists who are writing about him *at the very moment we are writing this* and will continue doing so for the next several decades.

We will simply add that while Trump is proud of having graduated from—his words—"the best school in the world," we wonder how proud Wharton is of having excreted this monstrosity.

---

* And "the women." And "the Mexicans."

# Benjamin Wadsworth

*BA, Harvard University ★ MA, Harvard University ★ Harvard University President*

With Benjamin Wadsworth, we reach the Ws in our alphabetical listing. The end is in sight—only seven monsters to go after this one. What's sad and distressing is not that there are still three remaining profilees who owned and/or trafficked in slaves, and another who was born too late to be a slaver but was still an out-and-out racist, but that there are countless others waiting in the wings, far too many to shoehorn into this compact* volume.

Wadsworth, the tenth president of Harvard (1725–1737), was one of three men known to have owned slaves while holding that distinguished post. He followed Increase Mather (father of **Cotton Mather**), the seventh Harvard president, and preceded **Edward Holyoke**, the eleventh. On the Harvard edifice that bears his name, Wadsworth House, where he lived with his wife and slaves, there is now a plaque commemorating those slaves, Titus and Venus, and Holyoke's slaves as well, Juba and Bilhah.

We'll leave it at that. Except, no. We won't leave it at that. We'll add that it's a puzzlement why Harvard didn't at least at some point expand its motto, "Lux et Veritas" ("Light and Truth"), to "Lux et Veritas et Servitutem" ("Light and Truth and Enslavement"). We'll leave it at *that*.

---

* And eminently giftable.

Except for one more detail about Benjamin Wadsworth. We quote from *Opposition and Intimidation: The Abortion Wars and Strategies of Political Harassment* by Alesha E. Doan:

> One of the earliest documents referring to abortion practices in America can be traced to a declaration written by Benjamin Wadsworth — future president of Harvard College — in 1712. He wrote that those responsible for contributing to an abortion, either directly or indirectly, were guilty of murder in God's eyes.

Leaving aside the issue of how he knew what was in God's eyes, it strikes us that Wadsworth's position was remarkably similar to that of many **Donald Trump** supporters in the Year of Our Lord 2017: antiabortion, pro-racial subjugation.*

Either Wadsworth was three hundred years ahead of his time or...

---

\* Overheard by a fly on the wall of the *Monsters of the Ivy League* office suite:
EW: Do we really want to say that Trump supporters are "pro-racial subjugation"?
SR: We're illustrating a point with an anachronism. We don't have slavery — racial subjugation — per se in the twenty-first century. But we do have racists, and which presidential candidate did those racists overwhelmingly support in 2016? So, yes, we can and *should* say that.
EW: I don't know...oh, all right.

# Dr. William Walker

*MD, University of Pennsylvania*

He was a doctor, a lawyer, a journalist, a warmonger, a slavery enthusiast, and, clearly, barking mad. Mad but not stupid. William Walker, born in Tennessee in 1824, graduated, summa, from the University of Nashville at the age of fourteen. Then on to study medicine at Edinburgh and Heidelberg, graduating with an MD from Penn. At nineteen! Practiced medicine in Philadelphia for a few nanoseconds before going for his law degree in New Orleans. After another handful of nanoseconds dedicated to the practice of law, he became the publisher of a New Orleans newspaper.

He also began a relationship with a woman who was not only a deaf mute but, soon, a dead deaf mute (cholera). Perhaps this drove him mad. Or perhaps it simply drove him from New Orleans. Or maybe he just wanted to avoid growing moss. In any case, at age twenty-five he rolled on to San Francisco. There, uncharacteristically, he didn't immediately start a new career, but continued with journalism for a while. On the side he evidently enjoyed quarreling: he was a protagonist, if that's the word, in three duels. He was wounded in two of them.

This should have tipped Walker off that gunplay was not his strong suit. Or perhaps it was the smell of gunpowder that truly drove him mad. Whatever. The important thing is, he soon reached the exciting, lunatic conclusion that what he required was *more* gunplay. Specifically, he got it into his head that what he needed to do was raise his own army, invade a bunch of Latin American nations, and establish colonies, under his personal control, in which English was the rule and slavery was cool.

It must be said that beating up on nearby Spanish-speaking nations was already in the air—a third of Mexico, or what we today refer to as "Texas," had recently been annexed by the USA—and mounting freelance invasions of other neighboring countries had become a fad.* So was the theory that God or Someone wanted the United States to keep growing, an idea that swanned around under the moniker "manifest destiny." Not that Walker needed all that to justify his plan. He didn't bother to justify anything. The man was bats.

In his first sortie, a scraggly little invasion of Mexico, Walker barely escaped with his life. That was in 1853. A couple of years later he tried Nicaragua, which, before trains, planes, automobiles, and the Panama Canal, provided a crucial overland link between the eastern states and booming California. In this round of his loopy scheme, Walker briefly succeeded: after forming an alliance with a faction in the target country, he got lucky, stumbled into a victory or two against feeble opponents, and found himself in charge of the ruling junta.

That didn't sit too well with his "subjects," not to mention with the governments of the other countries in the region, which launched an unremitting series of invasions. This inspired Walker to fake an election, declare himself president, and proclaim English Nicaragua's official language and slavery its preferred form of employment. People back home who followed the

---

* It was called "filibustering," unrelated to the current practice in which, for instance, Senator **Ted Cruz** stands at a lectern and spouts nonstop nonsense for more than twenty hours, causing his fellow senators to hate him even more than they had before. But we digress.

story were divided into two camps: those who considered Walker a criminal, and those who cherished slavery, detested speakers of Spanish, and idolized Walker, i.e., the nineteenth-century precursors of certain present-day troglodytes.

Walker's presidential reign was short-lived and inglorious. In May 1857, the US Navy nabbed him — rescued him, really — and brought him home. "That man," wrote President James Buchanan, "has done more injury to the commercial & political interests of the United States than any man living." Nonetheless, the government could not convict him of a crime, prevent him from drawing crowds of cheering idiots, or keep him from doing it all over again.

In 1860, after two more invasion attempts, Dr. Lawyer Journalist Walker, age thirty-six, was captured by the Royal Navy (yes, the Brits were also involved) and tossed like a hot potato to the Hondurans, who gave him a firsthand demonstration of the medical, legal, and journalistic consequences of being on the receiving end of a firing squad. He was buried in Honduras, where Spanish is the language and slavery was and is illegal.

Luckily for those who cherish the reputation of Penn Med, the Civil War came along, bumping Walker off the front page and nearly sending him down history's memory hole. Nearly, but not quite. "His bizarre career," says Pulitzer-winning historian T. J. Stiles (MA, MPhil, Columbia University), "would leave a legacy that shadows the relationship between the United States and Central America to this day."

Understandably. But it wasn't all in vain. Central American countries have historically lacked a defining War of Independence to celebrate. So they fixed on the 1856–1857 campaign against Walker as a substitute. Costa Rica, for example, made April 11 a national holiday in honor of his defeat. Three cheers! Or, okay, two. Okay, none. Is none enough?

# Lawrence Scott Ward

*Harvard University Assistant Professor ★ University of Pennsylvania Professor*

Lawrence Scott Ward has two Ivy League items on his CV. In 1970, at age twenty-eight, he was hired to teach marketing at Harvard Business School. In 1980 he moved to the Wharton School, at the University of Pennsylvania. Unlike other academic fields of study — Medieval Poetry, say, or History of the BeNeLux Nations, 1855–1911 — marketing is a discipline of which modern corporations can (or think they can) make profitable use. So Professor Ward was in demand as a corporate consultant, serving such blue-ribbon clients as Exxon, GM, and IBM. He anchored *The Wharton/Business Times Management Report* on then-new ESPN. He drove expensive sports cars and owned elegant homes in Cape Cod and *Maui*.

Not bad, for an egghead academic. But then, Professor Ward enjoyed two thriving careers.

No, wait. Three. He also enjoyed a thriving career as a pedophile. He preyed — if that's the word, and it is — on boys aged thirteen to sixteen from broken, desperate homes. Yes, he gave them and their parents money. He took some of them into his Main Line house — the one with the big surrounding wall that shielded their comings and goings from the neighbors — and insisted the boys go to school, or get a real job, or whatever. But the age of consent for adult sexual activity in Pennsylvania is sixteen, and these kids weren't that old.

Thus, in 1993 he was arrested in a sting — soliciting sex from

238

an undercover state trooper (who, despite his five o'clock shadow, looked like a teen). The prosecution brought two cases, one based on the sting, the other based on testimony from a young man who said he'd been abused. But a bungled wiretap and so-so evidence resulted, in 1999, in an acquittal on one charge and a guilty plea on two misdemeanors—attempting to promote prostitution and attempting to corrupt minors. Ward was sentenced (by a naïve, credulous judge) to five years' probation and a $2,500 fine—approximately what Ward the consultant earned in two hours.

Scott Ward continued his tripartite career for seven more years, until he returned from a three-week trip to South America, including a stop at Fortaleza, the northeastern Brazilian city notorious for its sex tourism trade. At customs at Dulles Airport, outside Washington, DC, an official noted an unusually large number of stamps from Thailand on the professor's passport. Need we tell you what Thailand, too, is notorious for? Oh, grow up.

The customs officials looked in his suitcase and found photos of Ward posing on a beach with kids. Ward explained his profession, how he studied "human behavior," and all that. Then they turned their attention to his laptop—on which they found videos of young children engaging in sexual activities, not to mention DVDs of Ward having sex with an underage boy. When police searched his office at Wharton, they found more than eighty images of Ward having sex with another boy.

He was arrested, charged with trafficking in child pornography, and in May 2008 found guilty and sentenced to fifteen years. In September 2009 he was sentenced to ten more years, this term stemming from additional federal charges of smuggling (i.e., mailing, to his office, from Maui and from Dulles Airport itself) still pictures and videos of himself having sex with a sixteen-year-old Brazilian boy. Ward also admitted to lying to US consular officials in Recife, Brazil, between March and August 2006, when he tried to get the boy, identified as J.D., a visa to enter the United States.

It's bad enough when priests do this sort of thing. What kind of society are we expected to have if marketing professors at Ivy League universities do it, too? There oughta be a law.

And there is.

# John White Webster

*BA, Harvard University* ★ *MD, Harvard University*
★ *Harvard University Professor*

He was born to a Boston Brahmin* family in 1793, so naturally
he went to Harvard. His father was an apothecary, which was
almost the same as being a doctor, so naturally he went to what
was then called the Massachusetts Medical College of Harvard
University. He traveled to London to continue his medical
studies and get some practical experience as a doctor, then to
the island of São Miguel in the Azores, where he practiced medicine, married the daughter of an official at the American con-
sulate, and made copious notes toward a travel and geological
guide,† all, in his words, within "several months...in the years
1817–18." A smart, interesting, busy guy.

Back in Boston, Webster set up a medical practice. Unfortunately, his income as a doctor didn't meet his expectations —
nor did the bequest he was left in his father's will — especially
since he and his wife anticipated having a family. (They eventually had four daughters.) Soon he switched careers, becoming a
lecturer and then a professor of geology, chemistry, and mineral-
ogy at his alma mater.

As a teacher, Webster was a "character." He favored pyro-

---

\* The term "Boston Brahmin" was coined in 1861 by Oliver Wendell Holmes, Sr. We
apologize if you feel betrayed or upset by our mildly anachronistic usage.

† Published in 1821. Here's the title in full: *Description of the Island of St. Michael, Com-
prising an Account of Its Geological Structure; with Remarks on the Other Azores or Western
Islands.* Actually, there's another line or two of title but our typographer quit.

technic displays in his lab (literally—he was called "Sky-Rocket Jack" by his students), and at least once was warned by the president of Harvard to lay off the fireworks. He could also be a live wire, if an occasionally ghoulish one, in his private life. Fellow professor Henry Wadsworth Longfellow told of how Webster once entertained his fellow guests at a dinner party by dimming the lights in the room, fitting a noose around his neck, starting a chemical fire in a bowl on the table, and, by the eerie glow of the flaming bowl, hanging his tongue out and making like a dying hanged man. A spectacle you would never forget had you been there—especially if you followed Webster's story to the bitter end.

For all his reported charm (ghoulish or otherwise) and intelligence, Webster had a serious problem: he couldn't figure out how to spend less than he earned. While he did make an effort to cut back—at one point selling his mansion in Cambridge and leasing a less grand place for his brood—he was still constantly in the hole. Aside from his desire to keep his ladies extravagantly outfitted, he was responsible for buying his classroom supplies, including the dramatic chemicals; he also bought an expensive mastodon skeleton, which Harvard still owns.

Webster's truly stupid solution was to borrow money from his friends. Enter Dr. George Parkman, another Boston Brahmin (although one who was actually rich) and Harvard-trained MD who no longer practiced medicine but had become a financier, moneylender, real estate developer, and slumlord.* Parkman and Webster had known each other since childhood and were Harvard classmates, so when Webster requested a loan Parkman—although notably thrifty—didn't hesitate. He was

---

* He walked the streets of Boston every day collecting rent from his tenement dwellers.

unaware that Webster was running a sort of Ponzi for Dummies scheme, borrowing from one friend to pay off another.

On November 23, 1849, Parkman visited Webster in his office at Harvard to collect on his debt. The historian Simon Schama, in his book *Dead Certainties: Unwarranted Speculations,* theorizes that it infuriated Parkman to learn that Webster had pledged the same item of collateral to him and another friend,* the two argued, and ... Parkman was never seen alive again.

Boston was abuzz with the case of the missing Brahmin. A week into the buzzing, the only witness to have seen Parkman enter Webster's office, a Harvard janitor, decided to take matters into his own hands. He broke into Webster's office and dug around until he found a deeply buried human pelvis and a couple of chunks of leg. (How, you ask, do you bury something in an office? You bury something in an office if it's a crappy little suite in the basement of the medical college, just next door to the janitor's crappy quarters. In ye crappie olde days, basements had, like, dirt floors or something. That's how.) The janitor promptly reported his discovery and Webster was arrested.

Boston went into shock. The trial was a sensation, covered by the national and even international press,† and 60,000 spectators flocked to the courthouse. *CSI* fans will be pleased to note that this was the first trial in which forensic evidence was used to identify a victim: a dentist testified that he had made a piece of dental work that was found in the furnace in which Webster had incinerated most of the rest of Parkman.

---

* I.e., Robert Gould Shaw. This was a truly stupid move: Webster certainly knew that Parkman and Shaw would occasionally converse. Why? Because Shaw was Parkman's brother-in-law and business partner.

† Charles Dickens heard about it in London. When he visited Boston in 1867 he discussed the case with Longfellow and visited the scene of the crime. His unfinished novel *The Mystery of Edwin Drood* has parallels to the Webster-Parkman story.

At first Webster proclaimed his innocence. In the face of the evidence, however, as well as a pitiful bid for clemency, he said it was self-defense: Parkman, his story went, had violently attacked him over the collateral screw-up, causing Webster to grab a stick and bat Parkman upside the head, killing him instantly. Then, out of "terrible and desperate necessity," Webster had to dismember the corpse and yackety-yak-yak. If he'd set out to kill Parkman, he said, of course he wouldn't have done it within the sacred precincts of Harvard. The jury was unsympathetic and sentenced him to death.

On August 30, 1850, Dr. John White Webster was — yes — hanged.

# Eleazar Wheelock

*BA, Yale University ★ Dartmouth College Founder*

Eleazar Wheelock had education in his DNA: his great-grandfather, in Dedham, Massachusetts, taught at the first free school in what would one day become the United States. Eleazar's parents owned a big, successful farm in Connecticut, where Eleazar was born in 1711. He graduated from Yale in 1733, procured his license to preach the following year, and preached away — to the choir and to everyone else within range — for the next thirty odd years. His claim to fame as a preacher was to train Occom,* a young Mohegan, to be a Christian missionary to other Native Americans in Connecticut and on Long Island. This inspired Wheelock to found a Christian school for Native Americans in Connecticut,† which in turn inspired him to dream of building his own college for the sons of colonists.

William Legge, the Second Earl of Dartmouth, had been a major donor to Wheelock's Indian‡ school. Like many aristocratic Brits, Lord Dartmouth felt a noblesse oblige to educate and Chris-

---

\* Not to be confused with the Franciscan friar William of Ockham, of razor fame, who died some 400 years earlier.

† The venture didn't go too well. Students tended to die of homesickness.

‡ That's the word they used back then, okay? Just chill.

tianize the savages. This philanthropic urge was so well known that there were times when members of a certain class of colonist, claiming to be seeking funds for the education of non-European North Americans, practically clogged the streets of London in search of highborn donors.

To encourage his patron's giving spirit, Wheelock named the new school, to be built in New Hampshire, Dartmouth College. As it turned out, Lord Dartmouth wanted nothing to do with the education of colonists; all he cared about was processing indigenous inhabitants into God-fearing Christians. Nevertheless, the name stuck.

According to *Ebony & Ivy: Race, Slavery, and the Troubled History of America's Universities,* by Craig Steven Wilder, Reverend Wheelock and his family arrived in Hanover, New Hampshire, with eight slaves, including a baby slave. That was more slaves than his school had faculty, trustees, and possibly even prospective students. Those slaves, except for the baby, must have come in handy when it was time to clear the forest for a civilized college campus in the wilds of New Hampshire.

As slave owners went, Eleazar Wheelock was far from the worst, and certainly not as bad as a later slave-owning Dartmouth president, **Nathan Lord.** Sure, over the years Wheelock developed an additional revenue stream buying and selling slaves. But, a) who didn't?, and b) he made especially creative use of them. For instance, Wheelock once lugged the body of a dead slave to an enormous pot he had behind his house, boiled the body until flesh had fully separated from bone, and wired the skeleton for use in the classroom.* Was this a colonial-era

---

* For further research: 1) Why did he own such a big pot? 2) What did he do with it after using it for this ghastly purpose? 3) Did he refer to this object as a "human" skeleton or as a "Negro" skeleton? If the former, mightn't that raise some sticky questions about the morality of slavery? And if the latter, what did he use for the former?

example of primitive recycling? Let's say yes. In any case, Dr. Wilder informs us that this was the beginning of science education at Dartmouth.

Eleazar Wheelock's lovely white house — once called the Mansion House — still stands, appropriately on West Wheelock Street. This is not its original location, nor was it Wheelock's original house. It was moved there in 1838 to make room for another campus building. Before erecting the Mansion House, the Wheelock family had made do with a log cabin.

After they moved into the big house, the cabin was repurposed as a dormitory for slaves.

# Woodrow Wilson

*BA, Princeton University* ★ *Princeton University Faculty*
★ *Princeton University President*

Woodrow Wilson! President of the United States! Winner of the Nobel Peace Prize for his work on the post–WWI peace process and the League of Nations! Big baseball fan, first president to go to a World Series game! Loved cars, went for a daily drive in a Pierce-Arrow *while he was president!* A progressive Democrat and champion of liberal reforms! Even halfheartedly backed women's suffrage! But wait! Before Wilson was president of the United States he was president of Princeton! A formidable fundraiser! Appointed one (1) Jew and one (1) Catholic to the faculty, where before there had been zero (0)! Raised admissions standards, instituted the novel concept of academic rigor, and started dismantling Princeton's image as a cushy playpen for lazy rich boys! What a guy!

Oh, yes, one more thing. He was a racist. A vicious, ugly, undisguised, unrepentant racist. At Princeton—the southernmost of the Ivies—Wilson promoted a "no blacks need apply" policy.* But that's the least of it: there were other colleges for black men to attend, most of them free of Princeton's ridiculous "eating club" culture. When Wilson became president of the entire country, he had the power to do damage on a vast scale.

---

* While Harvard and Yale had been admitting blacks for decades, not one (0—a shutout!) was admitted to Princeton during Wilson's reign.

In the decades after the Civil War, many thousands of qualified black men and women were employed by the government in good, secure, middle-class jobs. Some of them even had white people reporting to them. This was too much for the racists of America, who couldn't bear to think of former slaves and their descendants as human beings, much less as citizens, white-collar workers, or—heavens!—bosses.

Wilson, who screened the KKK extravaganza *Birth of a Nation* in the White House, fully subscribed to this point of view. In fact he had promised in his 1912 campaign that he would do his darndest to flush Negroes out of the government, or at least demote them to the lowest-paying, most menial jobs and enforce segregation (which he said was "not a humiliation but a benefit") throughout the government. It was a devastating blow, not only to those who lost their good jobs* and their place in the thriving black middle class—and who were forced to sell their houses, land, and possessions—but to their descendants. For generations. Discriminating against black people and providing affirmative action for white people: it was the official stance of the Wilson administration.

One finds oneself pondering various questions, e.g., why was Woodrow Wilson such a scumbag? Could it be that he was born in Virginia? That he lacked the imagination to rebel against his slave-owning, Confederacy-supporting parents? That he was the first southerner elected president since the Civil War and couldn't resist the urge to push the country back to the good old days, southern style? Don't ask us; we'll just ask more questions.

So, okay, there's this division or subset or interdisciplinary

---

* One example: it had been a Republican tradition to appoint black postmasters, especially in the South. This was a fine and respected job, especially compared to "slave." Wilson appointed whites to these—and all other—federal positions.

undergraduate-and-graduate program at Princeton called the Woodrow Wilson School of Public and International Affairs. Big prestige, best public-policy school in the world, if it does say so itself, hot-shit faculty, many accomplished alumni, and such as.* You can see where this is going, can't you? In November 2015, students occupied the office of Princeton's president† to demand that the racist's name be removed from the program as well as from a campus dorm complex.

In early 2016 the university announced that neither the school nor the complex would be renamed; rather, they would continue to be identified with the oozing pestilence known as Woodrow Wilson.‡ However, the administration swore that it would henceforth be extra honest about its history — and especially about that toxic slimebucket Woodrow Wilson. More important, steps would be taken to make the campus more welcoming to minorities; the school would actively recruit members of underrepresented groups to pursue PhDs; and Princeton would not only name various entities after people who contributed to the school's diversity but would hang pictures and, presumably, mount statues of them all over the campus.

---

* A reference to the famous and, in its own way, brilliant YouTube video of 2007's Miss Teen USA from South Carolina, which prominently features the phrase "and such as." South Carolina is a former Confederate state not too far from Wilson's native Virginia, which is all the justification we need for this non sequitur.

† Christopher L. Eisgruber, a JEW! Suck on that, Woodrow.

‡ It's not easy to change the name of a venerable, highly respected mandarin institution. There's just too much "brand equity" at stake. If it were to come out tomorrow that John Harvard had been a serial molester of young lady pilgrims and a slaughterer of baby harp seals, you can bet that the eponymous university would shrug it right off. But if, before his downfall, Bernie Madoff had handed $50 million to his alma mater, Hofstra, to establish the Bernard L. Madoff Institute of Financial Ethics, it's a dead certainty that the day after his arrest a crew of workers would have been rushed to the campus to chisel the sign off the building — either that, or to carve a hasty "Not" before the name.

# John Witherspoon

*Princeton University President*

John Witherspoon, a Scottish minister, was recruited in 1768 to become president and head professor of the College of New Jersey in Princeton, later known as...well, you know what it was later known as. The school was by no means a powerhouse of higher education. Its academics were pathetic, it had essentially no admissions criteria, the library was pitiful, and the school was too broke to do anything about any of it.

But Witherspoon was a gifted rainmaker, tapping donors both locally and in Scotland. He gave hundreds of his own books to the library. He instituted a Scottish-style rigorous academic structure. And he imposed admissions requirements that at least made a pretense of separating incoming wheat from chaff. The school quickly took its place among the leading New World academic institutions. Among Witherspoon's lasting contributions to American culture: he referred to his college's bucolic setting as a "campus," introducing the word into the American lexicon.

Being Scottish, Witherspoon had only a limited amount of patience for the English crown and was deeply involved in the American Revolution. He was a member of the New Jersey delegation to the Continental Congress and was both the only clergyman and the only college president to sign the Declaration of Independence. One slightly weird personal detail: at the age of sixty-eight Witherspoon married a twenty-four-year-old woman and had two more children on top of the ten he'd had with his first wife.*

So: a man of the cloth, fine college president, interesting fellow (a bit of a cradle robber, yes, but—dude!), important Revolutionary-era American. But if you've been with us so far, you probably know what comes next. Here we go. (Throat-clearing noises.) At his death in 1794, the inventory of John Witherspoon's possessions included two slaves, "valued at a hundred dollars each." That's right. This Protestant minister kept slaves while he was president of What Would One Day Be Princeton.

And here is either his defense or a blanket condemnation of the early leaders of Princeton. Witherspoon was the college's sixth president. The five before him and the two who followed also owned slaves. As did many of the trustees.

We'll go with blanket condemnation. And it's no excuse to say "Everyone did it." If everyone jumped off a moral cliff, would you jump off, too? So there you go. Thank you, and good night.

---

* Five of the first ten survived to adulthood, which wasn't too bad for back then.

# Elihu Yale

*Yale University Benefactor*

If you picture Elihu Yale, after whom the university was named, as an intellectual, or academic, or devotee of higher learning, or even as the founder of Yale, you're wrong.

Yale the person never laid eyes on Yale the institution. Born in Boston in 1649 to English-Welsh parents, he was whisked to Merrie Olde England when he was a tiny tyke and never came back. Which is not to say he never traveled. For much of his adult life he lived in exotic Madras, India — today's Chennai — where he worked for the British East India Company. He was appointed president of Madras and governor of Fort St. George. He had a wife, at least two mistresses, a vigorous entrepreneurial spirit, and few moral constraints. To supplement his salary he used company funds to buy land for himself, imposed high taxes on the natives, and made a fortune in the illicit diamond trade.

But why stop there? For generations Madras had been the hub of a vast slave trade linking Africa and Southeast Asia. Yale asked himself why he shouldn't get in on the action, and was unable to find a reason. So he and his colleagues — who, after all, ran the place — made a rule that no outgoing ship could leave port unless it was carrying at least ten slaves. Perhaps it was a matter of efficiency: with ten slaves you could sail in the maritime equivalent of the carpool lane. Or perhaps it was for other reasons. In any case, in a single month in 1687 more than 660 slaves were sent to the British colony on the island of St. Helena in the middle of the Atlantic Ocean.

It took almost three decades, but at a certain point the British East India Company had finally had it with Yale's shady/horrible practices. He was removed as governor, and in 1699 he returned to England, wealthy, respected, and famous — so famous, in fact, that his reputation (as a brilliant merchant, not a slaver or criminal) reached the pious Christian ears of **Cotton Mather** on the other side of the wide, wide Atlantic.

Mather, helping to launch Collegiate School in New Haven, wrote to Yale with a request for funding and a hint that, with a big enough gift, the donor's name might be slapped on something and thus immortalized. Yale went for it in a modest way, shipping nine bales of random stuff, 417 books, and a portrait of King George I. It doesn't sound like much to us — we give away portraits of George I in junk mail today — but back then the merch fetched around £800. The haul was enough to erect a single building. And lo, Yale College — that is, a building called "Yale College" that was to be part of a larger academic institution — was born. The name was later expanded to encompass the entire nascent institution, allegedly because the name of the person who was actually hands-on *responsible* for making it happen was Jeremiah Dummer, and the trustees would not countenance having their precious school go through life as Dummer College.*

Elihu Yale, no doubt flattered, attempted to leave the school a fat sum in his will. But it was not to be. After Yale died, Cath-

---

* Possible eighteenth-century vaudeville sketch:
MR. COSTELLO: Nice to meet you. I'm a Harvard graduate. And you?
MR. ABBOTT: I'm a Dummer man.
MR. COSTELLO: Well, obviously. But from what school?
MR. ABBOTT: The Dummer College!
MR. COSTELLO (slaps own face five times): I did hear you the first time! But which *one*, pray? What institution of higher learning did you attend?
(Etc.)

erine, his wife, still…let's say *miffed* about one or more of his affairs, took time off from her busy schedule of mourning and brought her case to the House of Lords. It worked! Boola boola! Fight fight fight! Bow wow wow! Eli's will was voided and the fortune stayed with her.

For years a portrait of the school's eponym, flanked by a dark-skinned servant wearing a metal slave collar, adorned a wall in Yale's Woodbridge Hall. Students complained, as students will do, and finally, in 2007, the administration deep-sixed the painting, stating officially that although Elihu Yale never personally owned slaves, they were relegating the thing to a storage room to avoid "confusion."*

---

* It's a real-life version of the old joke: Hymie has a barrel of herring. He sells it to Moishe. Moishe sells it to Isaac. Isaac sells it to Murray. Murray looks at it one day, decides he's a little hungry, opens it, and eats some of the herring. It's horrible! Spoiled rotten! Outraged, he calls up Isaac and says, "That herring you sold me, ptui! It stinks!" Isaac says, "Schmuck! It's not for eating. It's for *selling*." Thus with Mr. Yale's slaves. They weren't for having, or owning, or enslaving. They were for *selling*.

# Beneath Contempt

Some are born monsters, some achieve monstrosity, some have monstrousness thrust upon them, and others, while certainly not *un*monstrous, nonetheless sort of…

No! Please! Enough already! What we're trying to say is that it would be foolish to attempt a *complete* listing of Ivy League monsters; and writing a full-fledged entry for every monster on that complete list is, at least for this writing team, completely out of the question. Even if we wanted to do it, such an effort would have to consist of many volumes even bigger than this one! Either that, or printed in a typeface so small you'd need a powerful electron microscope to read it, which means it would be legible only to scientists in labs containing powerful electron microscopes, and, to be perfectly blunt, those people are not our audience. Our audience is you, dear, dear reader.

Where were we? Oh, right. Not to mention how long it would take and, consequently, how little we would make per hour, or decade, on the "every monster of the Ivy League, ever" project, despite its no doubt numerous personal satisfactions and social usefulness. Also, such a project, personal satisfactions aside, would kill us.

Anyway, as a compromise between what we've done thus far and the painful attempt to be completists, we present the following modest list of individuals we considered including but then decided: oh, fuck 'em.

Enjoy!

## John Ashcroft
*BA, Yale University*

Attorney general under **Bush Jr.**; creepy religious moralizer and culture warrior, distressingly awful singer-songwriter.

## Steve Bannon
*MBA, Harvard University*

Former Chairman of to-the-right-of-Fox Breitbart News. Now "senior counselor" to **President Donald Trump.** Enabler of anti-Semites and racists; right-wing hate merchant/ghoul.

## John Bolton
*BA, JD, Yale University*

Saddam/walrus-mustache-wearing neocon; **Bush Jr.** ambassador to the UN who hates the UN; chicken hawk who supported the Vietnam War but sat it out: "I confess I had no desire to die in a Southeast Asian rice paddy."

## Pat Buchanan
*MA, Columbia University*

"Paleoconservative"; former boss Dick Nixon said he was not a racist, anti-Semite, or bigot, confirming he is all of the above.

## George H. W. Bush
*BA, Yale University*

Promoted dull-normal Dan Quayle above his station; sired the Quayle-like diabolical blunderer **George W.**

## Dick Cheney
*Failed out of Yale University twice*

Vietnam chicken hawk ("I had other priorities in the '60s than military service"); coauthor of the Iraq shit-show; NRA poster boy for proving it's okay to shoot a friend in the face.

## Michael Chertoff
*BA, JD, Harvard University*

Bungling Katrina-era Homeland Security secretary under **Bush Jr.**; investigator on bullshit Senate Whitewater Committee.

## Monica Crowley
*PhD, Columbia University (if they let her keep it)*
Trump choice for senior director of strategic communications (read: liar-in-chief) of the National Security Council. Plagiarizer of multiple authors and journalists in her 2012 book, *What the (Bleep) Just Happened?*; plagiarizer of multiple actual historians in her 2000 PhD thesis (ironic opening of title: "Clearer Than Truth...").

## Thomas Davis
*MBA, Harvard University*
Former investment banker and pillar of the business establishment; provider of insider-trading tips to pay back his gambling debts; stealer of money from a charity; perjurer; in May 2016 pleaded guilty to 12 insider-trading felonies.

## Wickliffe Draper
*BA, Harvard University*
Nazi sympathizer; Pioneer Fund founder; funder of racist, anti-Semitic eugenics "research."

## Dinesh D'Souza
*BA, Dartmouth College*
Producer of mendacious right-wing propaganda films; convicted felon for illegal political contributions; hypocritical moralizer caught in a hotel room with girlfriend while a) still married, and b) president of a rinky-dink Christian college; ex-BF of **Ann Coulter.**

## John Eleuthère du Pont
*University of Pennsylvania dropout*
Du Pont heir depicted by Steve Carrell in *Foxcatcher;* threw his wife into a fireplace, choked her, menaced her with a knife, tried to push her out of a moving car, threatened to shoot her; racist; shot and murdered Olympic wrestler Mark Schultz.

## Louis Fieser
*PhD, Harvard University; Harvard University professor*
Invented the medieval-style weapon napalm in his secret lab at Harvard; "I have no right to judge the morality of napalm just because I invented it."

## Steve Forbes
*BA, Princeton University*
Goofy rich guy who persistently ran for president despite all indications that no one liked him or his "flat tax" economic scheme that rewards the rich, punishes the poor.

## Alberto Gonzales
*JD, Harvard University*
**Bush Jr.** White House lapdog, counsel, and attorney general happy to sign off on torture and anything else Bush and Cheney requested.

## James Kent
*Columbia University's very first law professor*
Slave owner; opponent of suffrage for free black people; gloried in the conquest of Native Americans: "the red men of the forest have…been supplanted by a much nobler race of beings of European blood."

## Jared Kushner
*BA, Harvard University*
Real estate heir, owner/ruiner of the *New York Observer*, husband of Ivanka Trump, *consigliere* to her father. A $2.5 million donation from his own daddy lubricated his acceptance to Harvard.

## Bill Maher
*BA, Cornell University*
Dogmatic, militantly uninformed antiscience babbler who promulgates on his TV show such shibboleths of the ignorant left as: vaccines cause autism, herbs and homeopathy are more effective than medicines, and GMOs are deadly.

## Reverend James Manning
*BA, Princeton University; Brown University's first president and first professor*
The Philadelphia Association of Baptist Churches sent him to Rhode Island to start a Baptist college. Arrived there in 1763 with his wife and their slave. Started a college.

260

**Megan McArdle**
*BA, University of Pennsylvania*
"Libertarian" propagandist for corporatist scumbags; devoted fan of Ayn Rand (blogged as "Jane Galt"); maker-up of "facts"; defender of Big Pharma because "innovation"; defender of plutocracy and privilege; user of Cuisinart to aerate *flour.*

**Michael Medved**
*BA, Yale University*
Right-wing radio-talker and literary overachiever; prissy moralist; smarmy defender of the free market, the "faith-based" life, and Mel Gibson's *The Passion of the Christ.*

**Mike Milken**
*MBA, University of Pennsylvania (Wharton)*
"Junk-bond king"; indicted on 98 counts of racketeering and fraud; paid $1.1 billion in fines and served 22 months in prison before acquiring philanthropic halo.

**Grover Norquist**
*BA, MBA, Harvard University*
Founder of Americans for Tax Reform; inventor of moronic "Taxpayer Protection Pledge" designed to make the lives of one percenters more pleasant; NRA board member.

**Bill O'Reilly**
*MPA, Harvard University*
Fox News propagandist, blowhard, bully; serial self-mythologizer; sexual harasser.

**Henry Paulson**
*MA, Dartmouth College; MBA, Harvard University*
As **Bush Jr.** secretary of the Treasury, he declared—in April 2007—that the economy was robust and healthy and the housing market "at or near bottom"— just before it crashed; named by *Time* as one of the top 25 people responsible for the financial crisis.

## Mitt Romney
*JD, MBA, Harvard University*
Strapper of pet dog to roof of car; layer-off of many workers after his leveraged buyouts stripped companies of assets and drove them out of business while his company profited handsomely; owner of offshore accounts; insulter of 47 percent of US population; casual proposer of "ten thousand bucks!" bet on national presidential "debate."

## Donald Rumsfeld
*BA, Princeton University*
Bush Jr. secretary of defense; coplanner of Iraq rat-fuck; torture maven.

## Stephen Schwarzman
*BA, Yale University; Yale University adjunct professor; MBA, Harvard University*
Tycoon-financier-businessman; chairman and CEO of the Blackstone Group; said of deal making, "I want war...I always think about what will kill off the other bidder"; said of Obama's plan to raise carried-interest taxes that it was comparable to Hitler's invasion of Poland.

## Ben Stein
*BA, Columbia University; JD, Yale University*
Nixon speechwriter; maniacal Nixon defender; once-ubiquitous show-biz droner (*Ferris Bueller*, game shows, et al.); product shill; dispenser of far-right commentary; proponent of "intelligent design" and other crackpot fabrications; abortion opponent; defender of sexual assaulter Dominique Strauss-Kahn, because economists don't commit violent crimes.

## Donald Trump, Jr.
*BS, University of Pennsylvania (Wharton)*
Sport-killer of endangered African species; ardent supporter of crazed fascist president; think *American Psycho*; alternatively, think *Uday* or *Qusay Hussein*.

## Ivanka Trump
*BS, University of Pennsylvania (Wharton)*
Socialite! Businesswoman! Model! Reality TV star! Author! Defendant in shoe-design-theft-lawsuit! Fervent supporter of her bigoted, deceitful, war-crazed, unhinged father!

## Sandy Weill
*BA, Cornell University*
Financial conglomerator who put together Citigroup (which the government buttressed with more than $45 billion to keep it from going belly-up during the Tribulations); vehement lobbyer against Glass-Steagall (which limited the risk banks could take); another *Time* choice as one of the top 25 people responsible for the financial crisis.

## Richard Whitney
*BA, Harvard University*
Yes, one of *those* Whitneys; president of the New York Stock Exchange in the early 1930s; a terrible investor and a bad gambler, he embezzled to cover his vast losses rather than trim his opulent lifestyle; served 40 months in Sing Sing.

## Paul Wolfowitz
*BA, Cornell University*
Deputy secretary of defense under **Bush Jr.**; the first Bushie neocon to suggest attacking Iraq after 9/11, and the hardest-core Iraq hawk of them all; primary author of the "Bush Doctrine" (essentially "We're the USA and we'll do whatever the fuck we want!"); nominated president of the World Bank by Bush, then forced to resign because he had an affair with a coworker (that began while he was married to someone else), plus other related scandals.

## Jeff Zucker
*BA, Harvard University; "Executive in Residence" at Columbia University*
Teflon-coated media failer-up and living embodiment of the Peter Principle; as president of NBC he signed **Donald Trump** for *The Apprentice*; almost destroyed NBC; now president of CNN Worldwide; current project: making CNN a permanent joke punch line.

# Eight Schools, One League

Seven of the eight Ivy League schools were founded before the American Revolution. They're old. Venerable. And rich.

Harvard is by far the oldest. It's also the richest—and we're not just talking a rich-for-an-American institution. We're talking the richest university in the world. It's peculiar, then, that wealthy alumni, and even wealthy nonalumni, appear to be in an endless contest to see who can stuff the most money into its nearly $40 billion endowment. There's a reason Harvard has been described as a hedge fund with a university attached.

What's true for Harvard is true to a lesser extent for its peers.* Associating oneself with Ivy League universities confers big-time status, which explains why insecure billionaires enjoy throwing money at them rather than funding other virtuous projects that could actually use their help. It explains why so many ambitious high school students go to heroic lengths to prepare what they imagine to be Ivy-worthy college application packages. And it's no surprise that a remarkable number of grown-up newsmakers feature a BA or graduate degree from an Ivy League school or two on their résumés: achievers don't stop achieving just because they reached the pinnacle of human achievement (acceptance to an Ivy) while still in high school. Needless to say, many of these ambitious newsmakers are not

---

* Should you decide you like this book so much that you want to write your own version of it, but without spending a lot of time on research, our hard-won advice is that you should—contrary to our foolish approach—call it *Monsters of Harvard* and forget about Dartmouth and Cornell and the rest of them. Your book will practically write itself!

the kinds of people you'd want your children to marry, unless you hate your children.

Herewith, your QuickStats™ for the eight Ivy League universities:

*Harvard University*
Cambridge, Massachusetts
Founded 1636
Motto: *Veritas* (Truth)
Body Count: Undergrads: 6,700; Grads: 15,250
Endowment: $37.6 billion
Went Coed: 1977

*Yale University*
New Haven, Connecticut
Founded 1701
Motto: *Lux et Veritas* (Light and Truth*)
Body Count: Undergrads: 5,453; Grads: 6,589
Endowment: $25.57 billion
Went Coed: 1969

*University of Pennsylvania*†
Philadelphia, Pennsylvania
Founded 1740‡

---

* One-upping Harvard's "Truth," because what good is truth if you don't have enough light to see it?

† Penn alumni face an ego deflating drip-drip-drip torture until the day they die. It goes something like this—at least once a month:
OTHER PARTY: So where did you go to college?
UPENN ALUM: Penn.
OTHER PARTY: Hey, go Nittany Lions! Penn State, rah rah rah! Too bad about that sex-abuse scandal. But really good school. (Etc.)

‡ Actually, 1749, but in 1899 the trustees "adjusted" it to 1740 for various technical reasons. The real reason: to scoop nearby rival Princeton.

Motto: *Laws Without Morals Are Useless*\*
Body Count: Undergrads: 10,406; Grads: 11,157
Endowment: $10.1 billion
Went Coed: 1880

*Princeton University*
Princeton, New Jersey
Founded 1746†
Motto: *Dei Sub Numine Viget* (Under God's Power She‡
Flourishes)
Body Count: Undergrads: 5,277; Grads: 2,697
Endowment: $22.72 billion
Went Coed: 1969

*Columbia University*
New York City, New York
Founded 1754
Motto: *In Lumine Tuo Videbimus Lumen* (In Thy Light Shall We
See Light§)
Body Count: Undergrads: 8,712; Grads, Professional, Medical:
22,605
Endowment: $9.64 billion
Went Coed: 1983

*Brown University*
Providence, Rhode Island
Founded 1764

---

\* Not great. But it's better than Columbia's.

† Princeton calls itself the fourth-oldest university in the nation (after Harvard, William and Mary, and Yale), ignoring Penn's 1740 claim.

‡ She who?

§ No shit, Jack.

Motto: *In Deo Speramus* (In God We Hope*)
Body Count: Undergrads: 6,320; Grads, Medical: 2,753
Endowment: $3.3 billion
Went Coed: 1971

*Dartmouth College*
Hanover, New Hampshire
Founded 1769
Motto: *Vox Clamantis in Deserto* (A Voice Crying Out in the
  Wilderness†)
Body Count: Undergrads: 4,200; Grads: 2,000
Endowment: $4.7 billion
Went Coed: 1971

*Cornell University*
Ithaca, New York
Founded 1865
Motto: *I would found an institution where any person can find instruction in any study.‡*
Body Count: Undergrads: 14,315; Grads: 5,265; Professional:
  2,324
Endowment: $6.03 billion
Went Coed: 1865 (coed at founding)

---

* Hope? Not Trust? What's that all about?

† Oh, my. Well, maybe all the other Latin words were taken.

‡ Yeah, no. That's a sentence, something Ezra Cornell said, something wishful and hopeful and nice, but it's no motto. Please try again.

# Acknowledgments

We thank the upstanding men and women of Wildfire for their gracious and enduring support, or whatever you want to call it:

Andy Aaron
Roz Chast
David Handelman
Ann Hodgman
Billy Kimball (ret.)
Patricia Marx
John Paul Newport
David Owen
Lynn Snowden Picket
Don Steinberg

We thank David Elliman and Mike Silverman for their monster suggestions.

# About the Authors

**Steve Radlauer** was born in Brooklyn before Brooklyn was cool. He is the author or coauthor of a bunch of books as well as a gaggle of articles for such varied publications (floppy things printed on paper) as *New York* magazine, *Spy*, *Esquire*, the *New York Times*, the *Los Angeles Times*, *Cosmopolitan*, *Asian Art News*, *Hamptons Country*, and the *Off The Wall Street Journal* and *Irrational Inquirer* parodies. He has worked in television as a writer and producer, is a founder of a travel-app developer, has been a creative on dozens of major-client advertising campaigns and an officer of two non-profit arts organizations, and was a restaurateur (The Ritz, Toronto) before people even *knew* the word "restaurateur." He did a considerable amount of his undergrad work at "Little Ivy" Union College and holds a BS degree from "Non Ivy" University of the State of New York. He and his wife, Kerry Willis, PhD, live in the famous borough of Manhattan.

**Ellis Weiner** was born and raised in Baltimore back when the Colts still played there. He has been an editor of *National Lampoon*, a columnist for *Spy*, and a contributor to four trillion magazines, back when they existed, including the still-extant *New Yorker*.

He enjoyed an extensive career as a writer for children's television until, for some reason, it stopped overnight. He has done a radio show dedicated to Brazilian music and has taught humor-writing at UCLA.

He is the author of numerous books and is the founder and editor-in-chief of *The Sherman Oaks Review of Books* (www .shermanoaksreview.com), an online humor magazine. He lives in Los Angeles with his wife, Barbara Davilman, and a continually changing array of dogs.

He is a graduate of the prestigious University of Pennsylvania.

**Randy Jones** (artist), as a child, could often be found on his family's farm in southwestern Ontario, sketching and doodling; there was never a question as to what he would pursue as a career. Leaving his rural roots, he attended an urban school that offered a comprehensive art program. There his gift flourished and he recognized that illustration and cartoons — historical, classical, political, social, satirical — were his favorite genres. His first commercial project was for the University of Toronto Press, followed by several years of editorial work for major Canadian newspapers and magazines. Eventually, he moved to New York City, where his talent and originality were quickly recognized and his work started appearing in the *National Lampoon,* the *New York Times,* the *Wall Street Journal,* the *Washington Post, Newsweek, Time, U.S. News & World Report,* and many other publications.